Proper Cornish Childhood

by

Michael John Darracott

Grosvenor House
Publishing Limited

This book is published by
Grosvenor House Publishing Ltd
28-30 High Street, Guildford, Surrey, GU1 3HY.
www.grosvenorhousepublishing.co.uk

A CIP record for this book
is available from the British Library

ISBN 978-1-906645-41-0

*With thanks to my son
Francis Darracott for helping
with the front cover*

If you enjoy this book, please take a look at my website below for future books I am in the process of writing.

www.Mikedarracott.com

In loving memory of my
Mother and Father
Georgina and Donald
Darracott

CHAPTER ONE

"Teeon Izza?"

Dad had just come home for lunch, and the familiar phrase rang out directed towards my mum, "Teeon izza?" meaning in Cornish (is the tea on), mum would be in the kitchen-preparing dad's lunch, with a freshly brewed pot of tea straight off the log-burning stove.

I am very elated today, because it's Saturday the 29th October 1966, and next Saturday is bon fire night. Dad had been occupied all week conveying stuff up from the local dump for our bon fire, the dump was just across the road from our cottage. We lived just up from Newlyn Coombe, in a beautiful cottage, set within a large garden.

The cottage we resided in back in the 60s, was called Trereife Lodge, and I am eternally grateful to the Le Grice family, for letting that beautiful cottage to our family. My father also worked for the Le Grice family, he maintained the greens, and hedges, to each side of the driveway, that lead to the manor. I quite frequently saw Charles Le Grice, conversing with my dad outside the cottage. Furthermore, quite often back then, I can remember my brother talking to Tim Le Grice. While writing my book,

1

I communicated with Tim Le Grice recently, to ask him consent, to write a little about our time at Trereife Lodge. So, I have written a little history here about Trereife manor house.

Trereife Manor house, has been the home of the Nicholls and the Le Grice families, since very early days, and the history of the house is never far removed from the fortunes of the two families. Architecturally it is one of the most interesting houses in Cornwall, and provides a good example of a house dating from the early 18th century, when the major part was built. A very large number of houses were built at this time, particularly nearer London, which exhibited a feeling for the symmetrical and beautiful.

Succeeding generations of the Le Grice family, have owned the house through changing times, when gradually the balance of prosperity and control, shifted from the countryside and the ownership of land, to the new urban areas. Over the centuries the house has increased in size, and architectural importance. The original farm house of the Nicholls family, was lower than the house as it now stands.

In recent times while bringing our own children up, my family delighted in fun days out at Trereife. Currently, Trereife house works closely with highly reputable local wedding professionals, to provide you with some wonderful packages for your Wedding. Among other things, they have a wonderful variety of farm animals for you to enjoy. In addition, a country kitchen serving up wonderful Cornish food. I would recommend that

Trereife House & Gardens, to be a lovely day out for all ages.

Anyway, back to 1966, we had a huge bon fire in the back garden, and dad had been buying new fireworks frequently, and adding them to an old biscuit tin for safe storage. I could hardly wait, but it was still a week to go, the tin was stuffed full of fireworks. My youngest sister Christine and myself, set about making our guy, we had lots of old newspapers that mum had collected for us, put aside. Mum had been saving all the old papers, and any other suitable stuffing material for ages. Christine and myself always enjoyed making our guy each year for the bonfire.

My sister was a few years younger, with me being at this moment 10 years old in 1966, so with my older sister Ann, and older brother Peter, being away a lot, I felt like a big brother looking after her. Ann my oldest sister was away a lot nursing in Truro, and Pete my big brother was also away a lot at sea, working on oil tankers. I missed them both so very much back then. I can still see Christine sitting with me, as we set about the construction of our guy, with her blonde hair shining in the autumn sun light. Christine would most likely be holding her teddy bear, a black and white one under her little arms.

By the end of that day, we had made a real nice plump guy, complete with a painted face, hat, and dad's old pipe. It would now be stored in the shed around the back of the cottage, until bonfire night. I loved the shed, it was like an Aladdin's cave of useful junk, harvested from the local dump by dad and Pete when he was home. You see dad had a trailer for his bicycle, he called it the butt, and the butt was used for every job you can imagine. Uses ranged From transporting logs for mum, or carrying treasure's from the local dump. One use included me!, you see dad had a Sunday job, he delivered the Sunday newspapers around Alverton estate, he would put the papers and me! In the butt, then I would give him the papers as he rode the bicycle to each home.

It was great fun sitting in the back of the butt, when it was a wet day, a waterproof cover, covered me from the rain, I use to laugh at being in the dark. Dad would puff and pant on the way up the first hill to the Rope Walk, and then whiz down the hill, to the shops. Next he would get me some sweets, Penny Arrows were my favourite, and black jacks. I can recall this one giant hill, Larrigen hill, that dad would belt down, and I would be hanging on for dear life. At the bottom, he would peddle along to a few houses around the boating lake in Wherry town, and then he would peddle back up through Love lane. Which brought us back into Alverton Estate, the two wheeled butt, I was in shook to the point, where I thought it may well fall apart.

While out with dad, mum would be busy baking home made pasties, and heavy cake, and jam tarts. Therefore, on arrival home, as we walked through the front door, the aroma of homemade freshly baked food, warmly greeted our sense's. It was the best fragrance you could meet with, after being out in the rain for hours. I cannot for a moment, ever forget the way my dad looked, after most trips out with him. He would Arrive back at home in his lengthy black mackintosh, dripping in rainwater, with his now well established trademark, of a dewdrop hanging from his nose. In addition, a half wet, half-finished, roll up cigarette hanging from his lips.

Having had our home cooked evening meal, I would now go to help dad bring in the log's, he had chopped up that day. I would place them by both the front room fire place, and the dining room wood burning stove. Then get into my pyjamas, and my dressing gown, in readiness for bed, now a kiss good night from mum, and up the wooden stairs. Once in bed dad would switch the lights off, but of course, as soon as he disappeared, I would switch them back on again. He would come back in and say, "You have got school tomorrow get some sleep", and then turn my lights off again. I then got my torch out and continued to read my comic under the sheets, until the batteries died.

Then its Monday morning, "Oh no", the sudden realisation as I am now awake, that it was back to school, had I done that homework?. I loved my school it was the best, I went to Alverton county primary school, which was just a short walk up the road. Furthermore, I cherished every single day, I was there, all the teachers back then were the best. It was so much more than a school, the teachers went out of their way to make you feel good, a credit to the headmaster, and all the staff. The food that was served was well yummy, and most of the dinner ladies who prepared it, were my friends mums.

I can recall going on a school nature ramble, the class were taken to a pond in a field, which to my astonishment was just a few yards from my back garden. We found newts and tadpoles, plus water boatman, all in this very small pond. Moreover, it was to be an originating point of my life long love for all animals. When I think back to lessons teachers taught us about beech nuts, and oak apples, trees, sycamore seeds and the reason they fly, it really fascinated me. They made everything magical and interesting, like the simple acorn, it could be made into so many things to state just one example.

After school I got mum and Christine, and took them to my newly discovered pond, my little zoo of little animals. I proudly told mum and Christine, all I had managed to take in, about the pond life from my school trip. We took some tadpoles back home with us, and I observed them grow into frogs over the coming days and weeks, and then despondently, had to return them to the pond. However, I maintained an eye on them every now and again, to make sure my babies were ok.

There was always so much me and my sister could do around the cottage, let me explain. We had four gardens, the back garden reached by a flight of steps, that are besides a waterfall. The waterfall came down the side of the steps, and then under the concrete path, and finally away to the woods across the road. Next the two side gardens, the first one was facing Alverton, and it was here I had my camp, set among the shrubs and small trees. The other side garden was facing Trereife House and is where Tibby first came on the scene. We had a pretty veranda on the front of the cottage, a great place to dodge the rain when playing outside. It was an adventure playground, a hide and seek paradise.

Inside the cottage we had even more areas to hide in or play, three bedrooms upstairs, a dining room, a living room, and a kitchen, with a bath and loo downstairs. Outside was another toilet, not forgetting of course the shed. I loved playing with my sister Christine, playing at pretend shops, and helping her make daisy chains, hide and seek was a great past time. I could live these days over again, a hundred times repeatedly. Many things were different in the 60s in comparison to today, we had many types of services to your door. I can recollect once a month, a man calling to sharpen mum's knives and scissors, he would bring a huge stone wheel, that he would sit besides. Next he would peddle the peddles, and sharpened the edge's of mum's kitchenware on the moving stone wheel.

We also had fresh fruit and vegetables delivered to our door, from off a horse and cart, from a gentleman who lived down Newlyn Coombe. You would hear him coming up the Coombe, the sound of the horses shoes against the tarmac of the road, could be heard while still quite a distance away. Mum would go out and decide on what she required off the back of the cart, while I stroked the horse. I loved the horse, he was so handsome, loving and gentle, and the man was a very cheerful chap.

I think it was the lifestyle that made the man so happy, what a glorious job he had. I use to run to the side of the road to watch them depart. The pair of them would have made a great picture for an artist to paint. A wonderful scene, as the horse and cart trundled back down towards the Coombe, over the newly fallen golden coloured autumnal leaves. This was much more fun than going to a supermarket to buy your fruit and vegetables.

One of my favourite jobs helping mum, was going down the Coombe and picking up chestnuts, ready for roasting on bon fire night, now only a few days away. Countless chestnut trees lined the Coombe, so it was a great job. I had to get to them though, before the squirrels did, and I was encircled by the little guy's most of the time. It was not so easy, I would be running around fast to get the big freshly fallen chestnuts, trying to outrun and beat a determined group of squirrels. I don't think the squirrels knew that there were hundreds of chestnuts on the ground, and that there was plenty to go around.

Nonetheless I succeeded most of the time, to get enough for mum on most trips, despite the competition with the squirrels. Around this time mum would also be making her pickle onions for Christmas, and I would help her in the kitchen as she also made the Christmas cake. Mums pickled onions were legendry, and just eating one would blow your head off so to speak, but they were nonetheless great. I use to help mum peel the skins of the onions, and "yes" it did make my eyes water, and the pickled onions made my backside burp!.

I can still remember mums old faithful pale mustard coloured earthenware bowl, that mum prepared the Christmas cake in. Christine and myself, clambered to beat each other at cleaning the bowl out, I won most of the time. The cake would then be put away, until it was ready for decorating with icing sugar and almond paste, and of course all the Christmas cake decorations. Best of all making the Christmas cake symbolized a more important thing to me, and that was Pete and Ann would be home soon. Pete and Ann would come back a few weeks before Christmas, and I looked forward to them both being home again so much.

With Peter hopefully back home soon for the Christmas break, I would be able to go back down to the woods to fish for the Big One. I could only go down to the woods, when my big brother Pete was home due to my age. Pete taught me how to fish for rainbow, and brown trout, and I loved it, there was not a lot Pete didn't know about fishing. There were many places along the river to fish, but there was only one place, to try to catch the evasive Big One. That special place was at the beginning of the river, as it passed by the refuse dump. On one of our fishing trips to this part of the riverbank, a while ago, the legendry big one got away, so we always commence fishing there first. The Big One had been caught at least three times, but had managed to wriggle himself off the hook.

On the arrival at the woods, the first thing Pete and myself would do, was to dig up some bait. We would dig up some worms, and Pete's eyes would light up if when digging, we found a maggot or two. You see maggots are considered to be the best bait, he told me for freshwater fishing. Next he would cast his line into the stream and the fast running water, would take the bait down to the spot where the big one resided. Anyway, for now I am observing mum prepare the cake and pickled onions for Christmas. While dad is outside stacking the bon fire high, in readiness for the rapidly approaching fifth of November, I was so happy.

With only one day to go to bonfire night, I managed to get an upset tummy while at school, so the school got hold of my mum, and to my surprise Pete came to pick me up. He had not only come home for bonfire night, but he was home until after Christmas, I couldn't stop thinking about all the fun Pete and myself would be sharing soon. I was so pleased when we got home and Pete said, "Mick if you're feeling better tomorrow, I will take you down to the woods," "try stopping me, I replied". My poorly stomach as if by magic by the end of that day had vanished, and I was now eagerly awaiting the fishing trip.

The next day Pete woke me up early, and we set off for the woods, we sat for 3 hours fishing for the big one in the pouring rain. We did not get one bite, so we set off downstream, and ended up close to Newlyn Bridge. We stopped to fish just up from St Peters church in fact, but we still could not get a bite. Therefore, we walked down to and over Newlyn Bridge, and went into Jelpert's ice cream shop. Jelpert's ice cream in my belief was and still remains, the best ice cream in the world.

My mum and dad had been buying this extremely delicious ice cream most weekends for as long as I can recall, Pete brought me a king size tub which was about a pint with a flake. We then both sat on the bridge tucking into our ice cream seeing the rain had now stopped. We must have looked like a pair of racehorses, with all the steam coming off our wet clothes, and then we moved to the pier to look at the harbour's activities.

I love Newlyn so many types of fishing vessel's, quite a few time's, I have dawdled along the North and South pier's and fished from both in all weather's, observing the vessel's, come and go. With seagull's swarming above them in hope of a free feed, I stare at them as they leave the harbour, and recall tales of pirate's Pete had told me. In the 1960s Newlyn was much the same as today, with Fishing its main industry, and of course a long history of artists, and art gallery's. To me Cornwall is the most wonderful place to live, I am proud to be Cornish and will never forget my root's.

In the distance I hear the familiar sound of conveyor belts coming from the South Pier, this conveyor belt was feeding stone into the holds of vessels, that are awaiting to transport it around the south coast I believe. The stone is coming out of the quarry, Penlee quarry, that's about a half mile away from here. The stone would be put through hoppers, and next the stone would be carried away by a lot of little locomotives, that pull along tilting carriages. The locomotives took the stone to the South pier, and then it was loaded onto a conveyor belt. The belt led to a chute that dropped onto the ships, and next the stone was then carried I think around the South coast.

I liked playing on the South pier even though dangerous, it would attract you to it like a moth to light, a recreation ground rather than a working place. When ever I was taken there I would soon be touching what I was told not to, just like any other child of my age would. There was bright red and bright green on and off buttons everywhere you looked. While noise and dust filled the air, mixed with a smell of fish, I was happy to play running in and out of the conveyor belts supports. Acting has if to be totally oblivious of any danger what so ever. Several captain's waved from aboard their ships to me, I use to imagine the adventure I would have if I was a captain or better still a pirate.

CHAPTER TWO

A Rat's Tale

Well later after our fishing trip and drying off we are now getting ready for one of my favourite nights, bonfire night but as usual it is still raining. Consequently I went to see what dad thought about the rain, he was in the shed organizing things for the evening ahead. I said "Dad, will we still be having a bonfire, or is it too wet", and he replied, "don't worry my cock, I will get it lit some how,". Dad always rubbed his hands together most of the time when talking to you, especially if happy, it was one of his trademarks so to speak. Mum was occupied making food for the evening ahead and Ann was home as well, great now my big sister and my big brother, were both home. I spent a few hours' carving out our pumpkins with Christine, huge they were, Jacko lanterns we called them, when finished mum handed us a candle each, and they were ready.

I spent the remainder of the day glancing out the window wishing for the rain to stop, and quizzing mum or dad if it was time yet. It always felt like an age waiting for the right time to light the bonfire. Then an air of anticipation ran through my body, as dad got up out of his chair, and put on his Wellington boots and went out to the shed. I accompanied him, "Are we ready dad?" and after a pause, came back, "No Michael, not yet, play with your sister", so back inside I went. He was just getting some paraffin ready to help light the fire, on account of the rain had drenched it.

Eventually, Dad came back in with an enormous tin of fireworks, and Peter and Ann then gave dad the fireworks they had both brought. Next mum called out for Christine and me to come and change into warmer clothing. We quickly put our heavy thick coats and our boots, gloves, and scarf on, and waited while mum got a torch. We now had so many fireworks and Christine was getting so excited, so was I, then it was time to go outside.

We went outside and up the steps to where dad was now endeavouring to light the fire, he was having a hard time trying to light it. Dad laced the bonfire with paraffin, and then heaved a match at it, repeatedly he did this, but it was very damp. At last it was alight sparks fleeing into the sky, thick black smoke curing our clothing as if we were kippers being smoked. Dad was walking around the bonfire with his pitchfork, gently caressing the ambers back into the centre. I watched the flames start to engulf our guy's arms, and soon he was well ablaze, and smoke was coming out of the top of his head. Next the sparklers, and soon Christine and myself were both making rings of fire and zigzags in the cold night sky, as we shook the sparklers around.

After the sparklers had finished, we went back down the steps to the back yard, dad then told everyone to stand back as he lit the first of the fireworks. The roman candle fizzed into life, throwing various coloured balls into the dark sky above. Suddenly, Mum gave out a huge scream, it gave Dad such a fright that he fell and knocked the lid off the firework tin. Furthermore, at that precise moment a single spark entered the tin, and the whole lot went up at once. Bangers going off six at a time, rockets flying along the ground at our feet, and jack in the boxes whizzing every where. I was dodging lots of fireballs from the roman candles, I was laughing to the point of near collapse.

Dads face was a real picture but even though fireworks were flying every where, he had time to ask mum what was wrong. Mum told him that she had seen the biggest rat ever walk right across the yard where we are stood. Next the rat came into sight, and dad went after it with a large Cornish shovel, dodging fireworks like a stuntman. The rat got away, but mum was right, it was a huge one. The fireworks had finished by now, and we were all coughing from the huge amount of smoke generated by so many going off at once.

By the time dad came back the whole tin had gone up, what a display that had been, not that we watched it mind, we spent the entire event dodging the fireworks while they appeared to attack us. I am sure the rat was sitting under some hedge nearby having a good laugh, but it was now over in a flash. However, we still had a pack of sparklers left, and also those days we had these unusual matches, that when struck glowed in all types of colours.

Poor dad, he was unmistakably broken hearted over it, but it was not his fault, he looked so sad and fed up.

I cuddled his legs and said, "never mind daddy, we can do it again next year", he looked down at me and gave me a reassuring smile, and then we all went back inside. That night I repeatedly got out of my bed, sneaking over to the window, trying to get a glimpse of the rat. I can remember being scared knowing it was huge, and that it may come up the drainpipe and bite me. The wind started to blow and my curtains started to move, I started to get scared and decided to call off my watch for the rat.

The next day I awakened to the sound of crows, living in the country it was a usual way to wake up, many of them lived right by our home. I believe this morning that maybe the seagulls have disturbed them. Squadrons of seagulls fly through daily in pursuit for food scraps maybe on the dump, at the bottom of the lane. However, this morning was different because I had heard a loud bang. I went into dad and mums bedroom and enquired what it was, I tugged at the blankets and dad woke up. Dad revealed it was just rabbit hunters and that their shotguns going off had disturbed the crows. From then on every time I heard a loud bang, I was sorrowful in the wisdom of knowing that perhaps a bunny had died.

With it being Sunday mum said we would be going down to the rock pools in Newlyn, to make up for a not so good bonfire night. I love the rock pools in Newlyn, we go down to them every summer, so it is a real treat to be going in November. Therefore, before very long Christine myself and mum set off for the beach and of course, mum brought us a Jelperts ice cream on the way past the shop.

We then took our selves and our ice creams to the beach, and then Christine and myself went to investigate the rock pools, with net in hand shrimps were soon in our buckets along with a crab or two. I use to love lifting small rocks up to see what skulked beneath it, I would spend hours on end turning rocks over. The pools we love to explore are just after the Tolcarne Inn, in front of the art gallery. With marvellous views of mounts Bay and of course St Michaels mount, which is accessible from Marazion. St Michaels Mount can be reached by using a causeway, that at low tide allows you to walk out to the Mount. Alternatively, you can go by boat from Marazion when the tide is in enough to allow you to.

Afterwards we wandered along Penzance promenade, mum always gave me some pennies to put in an old world war two mine that was on the promenade, it was collecting for charity, I believe. Next we brought some sweets which we eat while walking to Battery rocks, the locality for the Jubilee Bathing Pool. This art - deco lido pool was built in 1935, and access to Battery rocks is by utilizing a concrete pathway at the rear. The name Battery rocks came about from the fact, that in the 18th century a gun Battery was located where the pool is now located.

Just down the road a little from Battery rocks you will come across Penzance quay, home for both private and commercial shipping. It is the place for those who wish to travel to the Isles of Scilly by sea, will be able to commence from instead of using the helicopter based in Eastern green. With seafaring being a sizeable part of Penwiths past and present, it's no surprise to find a dry dock for marine engineering. You will find the dry dock besides the Ross swing bridge, work has been going on here since 1810. Behind that you will find St Mary's church, the largest church in Penzance.

Just across from the Jubilee Bathing pool is St Anthony gardens, and car park where in the not so distant future, my dad will eventually be working as a car park attendant. You will find behind the car park the place my dad enjoys a pint in, the Yacht Inn. The Yacht Inn is a delightful Inn, and yet another building in the art deco style of the 1930s. I have often listened to my dad speaking about how he had taken pleasure in downing a pint in the Yacht, during my childhood. It is such a beautiful building and the Yacht Inn offers traditional hospitality, and is a warm, friendly, comfortable Inn.

Well, after we finished our walk on the prom mum started to take us back home, halting at the boating pool in Wherrytown. Great, now I can sail my toy yacht a real beauty it was, it was rigged out with proper sails and rope like the real ones, I plopped it in the water and off it sailed. Then we had to wait for the best part of 20 minutes for it to come back, because the wind had suddenly dropped. We consumed the last of the lemonade that mum gets from sweet shops, back in the 60s you would buy lemonade powder and mix it with water. The boating pool is a fun place for me, it first opened in 1955 a year before I was born. If you walk right through it, it will take you to Alexandra Road. You can then cross the zebra crossing and continue to the fire station, and carry on from here to Morrob Road.

Now with our lemonade almost depleted, and all the luncheon meat sandwiches finished, it was growing a little dark and my stomach was growing hungry. Moreover, Christine was well nigh asleep on her feet, so mum gathered up everything, and we embarked on the walk back home. Trying for more sweets when we got to Newlyn, but of course justifiably, that was always going to be a non starter after everything we already had been given during the day. By the time we got to the bottom of Newlyn Coombe It was rather spooky walking in the dark. You could hear birds settling down for the night and Owls, but a full moon lit the pavement to our home. Arriving back home it was a bath and a early night, with school tomorrow, so I gave mum and dad a kiss and went to bed.

The following day at school I shared my firework extravaganza experience with my friends, and we had a good laugh about the rat. At least I could say that I in all probabilities had the best display ever, although one of the shortest. We all ran around the playground pretending to be a rocket and mimicking the sounds.

We all had to draw a picture of bonfire night, and I sketched the now infamous rat into my drawing, with my dad chasing after it, it was so funny. I still have graphic recollections of that night even now 42 years on. However, little did we know then that dad would die in just 7 years from now, from cancer reaching an age of just 47. This event would affect me for years to come and of course broke my heart.

Interesting in school today, our class like the others in our school were getting ready for Christmas. After returning from gathering pinecones from around Blue Bell Dell, we finished them off with silver paint, and then placed a plastic robin redbreast on the top of it. What fun it was back then cutting out snowflakes from paper, making Christmas crackers, and decorations. I loved all the outdoor activities the school took us on, all of us lined up teacher in front, and one bringing up the rear. Nature walks were my very favourite of all, it all added to the Christmas magic.

When arriving back home from school or at any time for that matter, Dad would always be working very hard, on this occasion he was busy carrying the logs in for the coming winter. The shed was almost full up as it was this time of the year. Most days on return from school dad would always have penny arrows and other sweets for Christine and me. I would get back from school and dad would put his hand in to his coat, and produce a handful of sweets like a magician.

I use to go out with my dad to help him bring the wood home from time to time, he would have a bow saw and a few sacks, in the back of the butt. Some times dad let me help him use the long saw an enormous saw, I had one end, he had the other, and we worked together. Not for long I hasten to add, I was only a little scrap of a lad, I did the best I could do to help dad. I can still see dad now, in a white shirt with the sleeves all rolled up over his biceps, His head running in sweat. Dad would cut himself now and then while sawing, and a mix of expletives would be whispered from under his breath. His best days were stormy ones because he could after gaining permission, go to collect wood that had fallen from trees during a stormy night.

One special day while playing by myself in the garden, from behind a bush came a faint meow. Next thing before my eyes was a beautiful little ball of fur, a black and white kitten. My pupils must have grown to the size of plates, and I reached out and picked him up. I took him to show mum and asked could I keep him, mum said she would have to ask around and if no one comes forward I could keep him.

Well, no one ever came searching for him, just as well, he was now called Tibby, and he was so loveable. He accompanied me every where, I played with him every day from the very first day. Every morning before my breakfast I would run down the stairs, and call his name through the back door. Within seconds he was there waiting for his breakfast, that mum let me prepare all by myself. I loved Tibby so much, and it's a marvel, he survived Christine and me with the amount of love, we bestowed on him. This little cat was still by my side 9 years later, I will never forget the times we shared.

The quantity of mice Tibby captured was amazing, but he never ever caught the notorious rat. When Pete and I came back from a fishing expedition, Tibby appeared to know that we had fresh trout, and would linger close by us anticipating a hand out. The little kitten knew that he had it good, fresh trout and affection from every one, he was a real part of my family. I lost this wonderful friend when I reached 19 years old, it was a very sad day for me. I cried for a week at the loss of my faithful loving cat, it broke my heart. He had a great life and a long life, I have not had a cat since.

CHAPTER THREE

The Snow Fridge

Winter is fast approaching now and its getting much colder, really hope we get a white Christmas, the last few days we have had sleet intermittently. I am Rehearsing my part in the school nativity, I am playing a shepherd this year, getting well excited can't wait for Christmas Eve. Every day on the way to school I drive mum mad practising my lines. Its only two weeks away Christmas now and the decorations will be put up this week, Christine and me always help mum to put the decorations on the Christmas tree.

After school mum took us to Alverton shops to buy homemade Christmas chains, Mum brought us four bundles each, we made them up very quick, on our return to home. They are fun to make you just lick the sticky bit to make a paper link, then join them all up. They come in assorted coloured strips and about 100 to a pack, after we made them, we put them away until time to hang them in our rooms. Tomorrow is the last day of school, and we break up for Christmas, and mum, dad, Pete, and Ann, are all coming to see me in the nativity.

I told mum about the lesson I had at our school today, it was all about St Michaels Mount in Mounts Bay. I learnt that it is accessible from the town of Marazion using the man made causeway at low tide. The island is made from a combination of granite and slate, and it is the official residence of Lord St levan. It has an array of old armour and other interesting antiquities, and scattered about are a few houses. Furthermore, it has a pier and chapel dating from the Fifteenth century, with many people visiting it each year. The castle tops it off what a superb place to visit, visitors to Penzance cannot fail to see it.

We go to Marazion beach every year in the summer among others of course, and it is extremely exciting to me having learnt a little about the history of the town. I read about one of the legends, about a ghost that appears on Marazion green. The legend says that people have seen a woman dressed in white that leaps up onto a horse, and sits behind the rider, and then they ride off into the night. It gives me goose bumps at the very thought of it, I hope I am not late one day going home from Marazion and see this apparition.

The Nativity went well and I am now thrilled over the snowfall last night, not much fell, but enough. Christine and I went out to build a snowman, armed with one of the old hats dads gave us, and a carrot for a nose we made a real beauty. Then I had an idea, I started to make a very big ball of snow and Christine helped me, next we hollowed out the centre. We got out some of our fruit gums and put them in the snow fridge. It was not long before they were twice as hard, and we were now the proud owners of our own fridge.

Its great to be able to play with snow, especially because it's not a regular sight living in the very far South West of Cornwall. Its so funny watching Tibby trying to work out what the white stuff on the floor is, I rolled a small snowball towards him to play with. The silly cat ended up licking the snowball but left it after a little while, I guess it was due to brain freeze. Tibby stands out very well in the pure white of snow, with his black and white fur, He's so gorgeous I love him so much.

Next we had Snowball fights and made snow angels, I got dad a real beauty as he came in from work with a snowball, I got one right back of course. I could smell the pasties baking and my tummy was anticipating every mouthful, not only that but freshly made lemon meringue for dessert. Tomorrow the Christmas tree will arrive, I always have great fun watching this. Mainly, because when dad cuts the string holding the trees branches, the branches fly out everywhere. I am so excited and It wont be very long now to Christmas, we are so close to the great day. I also overheard heard mum say that uncle Alf, and aunty Flo are coming tomorrow as well. They are the best aunty and uncle in the world.

In the morning mum took us to Penzance, and we went into my favourite store, and this department store is full with lots of toys. I was soon on the floor with Christine playing with any toy, that I could get my hands on. Then we bumped into Alf & Flo, they said they would be coming down to our cottage around teatime. They only lived about two miles if that from our home. On the way back from Penzance we stopped at St John's Hall to look at the Christmas tree outside. I remember my dad telling me that the building is completely made of granite. It is turning colder, so we get the bus back home, the Lands end bus stops near to our cottage so in no time at all were back home in front of the fire.

The snow on the road as all but gone, but our snow fridge and snowman still survive, but are both a little worse for wear. I wonder if we will get more snow, if so, I can repair our snowman who now looks past his sell by date, so to speak. After Alf and Flo have left, Pete takes me down to Newlyn. When we arrive in Newlyn Pete buys me a big bag of chips and a can of pop, we then walk on pass the fish market, and it's not long before were walking down along the South pier. As I wrote earlier I love this pier, with the large stone carrying ships awaiting their turn for another load. I suddenly turn towards a flash in the night sky, but not to worry it is just the light from an arc welder, who is occupied mending a ship.

The seagulls high above us appear like ghosts, when the blue light from the arc welder aluminates them. The surface of the sea shimmers and glitters, and the wind whips up the laying stone dust, that's laying on the harbour wall. The wind beats the rain into your face unforgivably and relentlessly, but look out fish nothing will stop us. We walk to the end of the pier, and can just see St Michaels Mount through a patch of fog. Its just about detectable to the eye from the tiny twinkle of a light from a dwelling there.

There is a beach that is just below the Red Lion Pub, that is a great place to dig for rag worms to use as bait. We go down regularly to dig there, but today we have mainly artificial lures. We finally arrive at the spot by the light-house, that we will fish tonight. Due to the fog a very loud fog horn will blast out throughout the night, quite frequently I might add. Since we are actually leaning against the lighthouse, the fog horn deafens us the whole time were there.

Pete lets rip a Long cast with his fishing rod, and our eager eyes await the float bobbing in the sea to disappear. Winding in the line every now and again due to passing boats, Pete gets a bite and becomes lively, will the fish win? Unfortunately, the fish wriggles off the hook. My hands are getting well cold by now, and I keep them inserted in my pockets, I am glad I wore my hat and scarf mum had required me to take. I also had few winter mixture sweets in my pocket which I eat in a useless attempt to keep warm.

I now delve into my back pack to get a ham roll because the cold always makes me so hungry, the wind starts to make my eyes water, and my lips to dry out. I wonder how much longer Pete will continue to fish, but don't ask because I do so want to catch a fish. Suddenly, the darkness is lit up with the passing of a huge trawler that's coming back after a trip. The deck is a hive of activity, and I watch it slowly moor up over by the fish market.

By now at least four other people have joined us, Pete prompts me frequently to be careful because it is a very long drop. I know the tides are strong here so I always kept well back from the edge. We managed to catch some whiting, pouting, and mackerel by the end of the night. Now we have had enough and head for home, when we got back Pete washed and refrigerated our catch. Tibby waited besides Pete for the offal from the fish, and the moment Pete put it in the bowl Tibby ate it in seconds.

The best part of coming back late and cold was the blast of warm air that greeted you, this came from the heating within that engulfed you when opening the front door. Next a hot drink and bath, a bit of television, I was allowed to be up longer due to the holidays. Some of my favourite shows back then were Dr Who, Muffin the Mule, Blue Peter, The Saint, Andy Pandy, Crossroads, Top Of The Pops, Dixon of Dock Green, to name but a few.

The next day mums busy getting the washing done while dads busy cutting up logs, I help dad by putting the chopped logs into sacks. I get to have a go at manufacturing kindling, dads gives me the chisel and hammer, and then places the chisel on to the wood. I hit the wood hard, and soon I am making lots of kindle. I feel very fulfilled to have learnt another of dads chores, I feel like a big boy like my brother Peter. Dad tells me that I have done a great job and gives me my own hammer and chisel, and told me that I can use them when ever he needs me to help him.

In the afternoon Christine and I have a game of hide and seek together, I can see Christine pretending not to look while I find a convenient hiding place, one eye peeping through her fingers. "Coming ready or not", she called out to me, I use to change position a lot so I always got a longer go. Dad once again had stopped what he had been doing to speak to someone who had managed to get lost. We live on the main road to Lands End, and quite a lot of tourist traffic passes by our cottage.

I lost count of the many people who came to our front gate, asking for directions to Lands End, of course I always went and got dad or mum. Cars frequently pulled up and tourists would ask dad the best way to go. Dad would always oblige them with his local knowledge, and they would soon be on the right track. Quite a few times they came back our way and gave dad thanks for his help. It was a very pleasant lifestyle living in the country with all its beauty. There were an abundance of animals to be seen, many around our cottage, and even more in the back field.

The wildlife around my home included rabbits, badgers, robins, thrush, black bird and crows, hedgehogs, and mice, and were all common visitors to our garden. We also had frogs and toads living along and in our waterfall, it was so rich in nature and so beautiful. I have always enjoyed and loved wild life and living in the country, and I accredit this fondness to my childhood. I have a great affinity with animals, all my life since living in the country I have noticed that a lot of animals I come in contact with, seem to enjoy my company, I guess that sounds silly, but it is true. I can approach any cat or dog, or wildlife and in no time build a trusting relationship in a matter of minutes. Dad came Back in and said that the people he had spoken to, had been searching for St Just and had lost their bearings.

Later I took out my special tin of cherished tea cards, my mum and dad gave me the cards that came with the tea.

Among the collections of tea cards, I had the following sets, transport through the ages, mans first 50 steps into the universe, trees in Britain, and the history of the motor car. At the very bottom of the tin was my prize collection, these are my world cup 1966-football medals, and these, I had given to me by my uncle. They are commemorating the match of England v Germany, and of course we won. My uncle got them when buying petrol for his car, and every now and again when he came to see us, he would hand over a load of these medals to me. I also kept my catapult and best pea shooter in there, away from my mum and dads eyes.

Another treasure fond to me was the 1966-world cup book souvenir, also acquired when buying tea. Over the years I lost all of these things, and I reckon they would be worth a small fortune by now. Furthermore, I had several large toy boxes all of which were absolutely overflowing with toys. Christine and I were content to play with each other's toys together, my toy soldiers would go and rescue her dolls, as if they had been entrapped in some war torn country. My sister would dress in her nurse's outfit, and my toy soldiers would bring back her injured dolls for her to fix up. I enjoyed playing with our toys together, it was an enchanting time and ageless in my mind. Tibby my over loved cat spent most of his time playing alongside us, and I do not think he ever stopped purring. Tibby of course was happy with just a small piece of string being dangled in front of him.

While playing in the garden I came across a lifeless blackbird, I had my dad look at the bird, but it was unquestionably dead. It was sad to think that the poor bird never got the chance, to be took to the wild bird sanctuary in Mousehole. This bird hospital, that I will now tell you about, is a renowned one and will be found halfway up Raginnis Hill. The hospital was originally founded in 1928 by the Misses Dorothy, and Phyllis Yglesias. In those early days, the hospital was originally named The Jackdaws hospital, but was eventually however, changed to the Mousehole Wild Bird Hospital & Sanctuary. Eventually, it would not just look after Jackdaws and other wild birds, but would actually care for injured Gulls, and other sea birds.

My brother Peter and Ann had both taken me there quite a few times, and I was mesmerised at the site of all the birds. I can remember that you'd climb a flight of steps and once at the top, you'd ring a bell that hung from a rope. Upon hearing the bell a person would come out and take the injured bird you had brought, into the sanctuary for an evaluation. The work they did and still do is just incredible and is a credit to them, and the Misses, Dorothy and Phyllis Yglesias. This sanctuary is amazing they take in sick and injured birds and baby birds, from all over Cornwall and beyond, they nurture them, and feed them, until hopefully well enough to go back into the wild. If not well enough to go back to the wild the birds will get sanctuary for the rest of their lives.

On my many visits to Mousehole I would see fit seagulls, and wild birds flying around high up above the pens, looking down at the sick birds. The fit gulls and other birds, would many times attempt to land on the pens and cages in hope of a free feed. While in Mousehole looking out towards the sea you can see a small island, its Mousehole island. Many gulls can be seen here roosting and nesting, also to be seen are terns, shags, gannets, razorbill, guillemots, and oystercatchers to name but a few. Grey Seals are seen frequently leaving the sea heading for a beach. Actually, around the year many marine animals can be found in our Cornish waters, such as bottlenose dolphins, and porpoises. Many will also be found visiting a Cornish harbour and bays around our coastline.

The wildlife we have in West Cornwall due to our climate is quite staggering, so I will list but a few here. We have badgers, rabbits, bats, frogs and toads, seagulls, dragonflies and damselflies, butterflies and moths in abundance. In addition, I have seen grey squirrels and hedgehogs, fox, moles, and of course the Adder to name just a few. Meanwhile in Trereife Woods I have personally seen many times, river otter swimming up and down the river and resting on the river bank. I love all animals and consider myself, to be a very lucky boy to be able to live among so many beautiful creatures. Cornwall offers an impressive amount of wildlife, and its so easy to find them all, if you know where to look.

With regards to our coastal birds here in Cornwall, here are some, I have seen, the Curlew, Little Egret, Oyster Catcher, Mute Swan, Shag, Ring Plover, black back gull, Kingfisher. Among our land birds so to speak are robin, blackbird, thrush, wren, crow, kestrel, sparrow, starling, swallow, wagtail, blue tit, and many more. I will not attempt to list all the birds we see here in Cornwall, but I hope I have conveyed a little of the wonder that I see with my eyes.

In addition to Cornwalls wildlife there is also a huge amount of Flora found on many of the footpaths, bridle ways, byways, and lanes. Just walk along any rugged cliff top and marvel at the bays, coves and the sandy beaches below you. Ingest the fresh coastal breeze into your lungs, and while stopping for refreshment maybe enjoy a Cornish pasty. Walking the many coastal paths around Cornwall you will find depending on the season of the year, Cowslip, wild Angelica, Foxglove, onion flower, Red Clover, Honeysuckle, Red Campion, Poppy, Burdock, Scentless Camomile, Gorse, Celandine, Evening Primrose, Ragwort, and these are just a few.

West Cornwall is one of the best walking locations in England in my opinion, and there are so many walks to discover here. Furthermore, while standing on a path upon a cliff top, I know of nothing more awe-inspiring that will top looking out to sea, from such a beautiful vantage point. Cornwall is a wonderful remarkable place, and it gives inspiration to so many, and it's no surprise that so many people return here every year for a holiday.

Anyway, getting back to when I handed dad the dead bird, he disposed of it, and its time for tea now. Christine and myself join mum in the kitchen and the aroma of mums delicious stew and dumplings fill the air. In addition, mums made another favourite of mine, treacle tart. I gobbled up a plate of stew hardly chewing, in anticipation of the Treacle tart. Then paused before picking up a slice Because mum shouted, "more stew Michael?". Of course, a second helping of mums stew was a suitable enticement for me to wait for a little longer for my treacle tart. Afterwards I tell mum I have indigestion and mums not surprised due to the speed I ate my meal, mums nickname for me is Two Belly's.

Tomorrow dad will be putting up all the Christmas decorations, including the homemade ones Christine and myself made. Our first job in the morning will be to go out in the garden and find a nice piece of holly, with lots of red berries to go above the fireplace. Before I went to bed, I went and sat with dad in the kitchen I asked if he wanted to help Christine and me to get some holly tomorrow. Dad told me he had to go to work tomorrow, and after he was going to put up the overhead decorations, when he came home. My reply was that when I grow up, I hope I am rich, so he would not have to work hard any more. Dad then told me the following, "The world owes you a living son, but you have to work hard to collect it".

CHAPTER FOUR

The Sack Hunt

Awaking the next day to a chorus of blackbirds singing, I am so happy and excited with it just being a few days to go to Christmas. I have a few pieces of toast for breakfast, mum had brought the bread from the Co-op store. The breads wrapper had pictures of Cornish Choughs, fishing boats, miners, and fishermen at this moment in time, printed on it. The bread wrapper had the words, Bara An Gwella Dyworth Kernow!, which I recall meant the best bread from Cornwall!

After breakfast I head off for the garden with Christine to find some holly for mum, and we find some very nice pieces for placing above the fireplace. Dad is busy working on the general Christmas decorations, and mum is kneeling down by the Christmas tree sorting out the baubles. We join mum and start passing her the decorations, while dad lifts Christine up to enable her to put the fairy on the top of the tree. Next after mum finished positioning the decorations on the tree, dad is putting the Christmas tree lights all over it, then a little count down, "3 - 2 - 1" and "hooray" the tree is lit up beautifully.

Christine and I are buzzing with excitement, and we go up stairs to finish off our letters to Santa. They are very big letters, Not to worry I think to myself Santa will deliver my huge wish list, well hopefully. I help Christine with hers after I finish my own, and then we give them to dad to keep until Christmas Eve. Every year on Christmas Eve, dad puts our lists in the fire and then the sparks transports our wishes up to Santa. The best bit is on Christmas day upon awaking, we have a lot of fun doing a Christmas sack hunt.

Its now late afternoon and I play with Tibby on the back lawn, he loves running after a long piece of grass, which I am pulling along the ground for him. It is so funny to watch him suddenly lose interest in chasing the grass, now in favour of chasing grasshoppers that presented in front of him. In addition, all at once it seems the garden is alive with grasshoppers all trying to flee Tibby, who to them must look like a tiger. I pick him up and give him a great big hug, I love Tibby so much he is one of my best friends. He purrs with content, whilst I carry him in door's to give him a bowl of milk. Well, its time for a bath and then a bit of telly, and then to bed, for tomorrow is Christmas Eve.

Today the smell of roast pork and beef cooking awakens me, mums got up early, and is setting about cooking the meat for Christmas Eve supper for later. After breakfast we join mum in the kitchen helping her to make mince pies, and sausage rolls. The coal man comes to the door with the Christmas delivery, and dad gives him a handsome tip. Next mums placing silver sixpences in the Christmas pudding, hope I am lucky enough to get one on Christmas day.

My Dad then brings out three crates of fizzy pop, and mums bring down an enormous amount of chocolates and sweets, that she had been hiding from us. Next, a load of fruit and vegetables are delivered, the front room is awash with sweets and chocolates, monkey nuts, fruit, and dates. Our eyes are popping out our of our heads, while mum struggles for space in the kitchen trying to store all the extra food.

Mum then gives Christine and me our first taste of Christmas, a hot mince pie, and a few sausage rolls, fantastic I love this time of the year. I am so excited at every single Christmas thing, everything about Christmas makes my whole body quiver with excitement. The way my mum and dad did Christmas for us, was magical, and I will never forget my childhood Christmas's. It is now the time I have been waiting for all year, it is the trip to Mousehole for the Christmas lights, one of my favourites for Christmas, and I relish every moment of it.

Now we set off for Newlyn and a fish and chip supper, and then onwards to Mousehole, and by the time we arrive there its already very crowded. The Christmas lights held here every year are truly amazing, and these days as I write this book, folk come in thousands to see them. Mousehole pronounced Mauzal is a village and fishing port, and as been holding the famous Christmas lights for over 40 years at the time I am writing this. It is really in every sense of the word spectacular, and I love going there every year. Please remember to give generously to the charity that helps to keep the lights year in year out.

It the best night ever with the Christmas lights all twinkling, people are singing Christmas carols, and it's a magic evening. The lights reflections, dance out across the water in the harbour its so very pretty. We walk around to the other side stopping occasionally to look into art and craft shops among others. Happy people are everywhere you look and the smell of mulled wine wafts through the streets. The odd Gull hovers quite high above us probably due to the noise from below that as disturbed his sleep.

We walk past the famous Ship inn which dates back at least 400 years, the owners gave me permission to use a picture of the Inn on the front cover. Every year the ship inn on the 23rd December celebrates Tom Bawcock's Eve. Tom Bawcock's Eve is a festival and memorial to Bawcock for his effort against a famine, the legend says a great storm kept local fishermen from going to sea. Therefore, Tom the legend goes risked his life going out to sea to fish, and indeed caught enough fish to feed the entire village.

The fish Tom Bawcock caught were used to make a pie, and the name of this creation is the "Stargazy pie". Furthermore, every year in the Ship inn they prepare this famous pie, and many villagers and visitors celebrate the tradition, it is a wonderful night and a very busy night. The Ship inn is a delightful inn with its real ales, very good wines, and a menu that makes use of local produce. Mousehole has a beautiful harbour with little winding roads, amidst shops and cottages surrounding it. The Christmas lights set within the backdrop of Mousehole, is an amazing sight and is a great achievement for the village. I for one enjoyed my Childhood

Christmas experiences just that little bit more, thanks to the Mousehole lights each year.

We carry on walking around the harbour, stopping occasionally to look at artist's work in nearby galleries and pottery shops. Dad gives Christine and myself a bag of sweets each, that he had concealed from us all night and a bottle of pop. Then down to the harbour where along little paths that run along the edge, boats will be found on dry land. I look inside some and imagine how hard it is to go out fishing in all weather. Christine and I can see the tide is out enough to reveal a small piece of beach, so we go down and scrape around in the sand for shells. We find an array of shells down there and Christine picks up quite a lot of them, and then it is back up to the path, where mum now puts Christine's shells into her handbag.

You can hear carols from around the harbour and occasionally a Sea Gull flies into view, as if to do its own tour of the Christmas lights. My sister is Skipping along the path singing jingle bells, its nearly Santa time, I think to myself. Next, a huge rush of excitement hits me, I say to Christine "not long now, and she gives me an enormous wide smile in acknowledgement.

We now stop walking around the harbour and just take one last look, with total gratification at the view we see each year. The twinkling Lights dance along in the night and I look to the sky and dream of Santa coming. Not long now I think to myself, soon mum will be reading The night before Christmas to us. That is the absolute last thing I hear before my eyes finally close on Christmas Eve. That time is still a few hours away, as we sit and take in just a few more moments of Mousehole's stunning Christmas lights. Then dad and mum indicate its time to leave, and we head towards the bus stop. My heart quickens with the thought of Santa who will soon be coming down our chimney.

Arriving back at home we tuck into a cold meat supper, absolutely delightful with mums homemade pickled onions and salad. Next we must put a carrot, a mince pie, and a little milk, besides the fireplace that's intended for refreshment for Santa. He will be very tired by the time he gets to our home, and clambers down our chimney pot. Now mum sits us besides her and reads the night before Christmas to us. Next were off to bed, and I get up throughout the night checking if Santa as been, and ultimately fall asleep having found nothing or no one in my bedroom.

Its Christmas day, I get up run into Christine's room with my Christmas stocking in hand. Christine awakes and gets her stocking, "come on Christine! It's Christmas day!" and off we run down stairs probing room after room. All of a sudden, I find a huge pile of sacks all filled to the brim with presents behind the settee. Mum helps us to drag all of the sacks to the front, I find four sacks with my name on them. My eyes are like saucers and my heart is thumping, Christine is already tearing open her first present, so I wait, and then we open our presents in turn. Christine has a selection box now my turn, "wow" a toy garage and cars, this goes on in turn for nearly a full hour until all our sacks are empty. Then we finish off by looking in our Christmas stockings, that had been forgotten about in the rush to find the sacks.

Now looking at my presents one by one, first, I examine a large robot I have, I turn his switch on, and he starts to walk forward next a panel on his chest opens, and spits lots of sparks out. Awesome, then I notice he has a series of buttons to push that release missiles, fantastic, I shoot one off in Christine's direction. Next I turn my attentions to a slide projector and slides I have. However, I put it to one side when I find a rocket, I turn it on and it dashes across the floor and then stops, it makes a loud siren sound and then stands to a vertical position. I also have a Donald duck glove puppet, it will complement the other puppets I have. I show it to Christine, and she laughs because we had seen Donald duck on television only the other day.

We both have lots of toys and are so very happy, we are also half way through eating our entire Christmas selection boxes. My stomach is turning a bit, and if I eat any more chocolate I think it will explode. We play all morning together Christine and me, sharing our toys, I give Christine a row of my toy soldiers and a few cannons, and we have a war against each other. Our cannons fire matchsticks, blank matchsticks, dad joins us for a moment, and he is well happy. Its so nice to see mum and dad enjoying their selves, instead of working hard like they normally do.

Time flew by, next mum calls us all in to the dining room for Christmas lunch, and the table is dressed so beautifully with a big red spiral candle, and Santa serviettes. Then mum brings in the turkey and all the vegetables, its remarkable I still have room for this feast. Next, the Christmas crackers, just as I was about to pull one with

Christine, I had to duck from a flying cork that dad liberated from the sparkling wine bottle. It missed me but left a small impression on the ceiling above, we all laughed so much while dad looked about the floor for the cork. Next, each of us one by one read out the jokes from each of our crackers, while we all sat with our paper hats on, playing with the little toy from our crackers, eagerly swapping any toy we didn't like.

After our main meal dad brings in the Christmas pudding, it is on fire with brandy burning on top. I think the pudding being set on fire is amazing, actually the whole of Christmas is, in addition this year I did get a silver sixpence in my pudding. Everyone is so happy dads enjoying that rum stuff, and Ann and Pete are playing with Christine and me, which is really nice seeing we don't see them that often.

Ann reads to Christine some fairy tales from Christine's new book while Pete shows me how to use my new slide projector. Later I give Christine a film show in the hallway, its darker there, and I can also use the back of the door as a screen. Christine sits down with me, and I switch on my new projector, and then we both enjoy viewing slides of, snow white, and Donald duck to name but a few.

Later on I listen to Christine's new record player, I can remember hearing Yogi bear songs and nursery rhymes. I still remember the start of Christine's Yogi bear song to this very day, it started "Yellowstone park was dismal and dark before Yogi". We also played with her building blocks, we played all the way up to teatime. Now, we are once again called to sit at the dining table, where I eat some sausage rolls, Mince pies, Christmas cake, and pull a fresh batch of crackers. Next, Another big favourite of mine, board games, snakes and ladders, and a whole multitude of other games. By the time Christine and I go to bed, we are absolutely exhausted and Boxing Day is just a one night sleep away.

Boxing Day is a complete rerun of Christmas day for us, and the coming few days are just the same as well. In fact, to be honest from Christmas Eve to around the 28th December, our parents succeed to keep every day as fresh as Christmas day. Moreover, they do this year in year out, mum and dad's commitment to a happy Christmas is phenomenal. Furthermore, now that I am older I realise the sacrifices they made for us all. I love them both so very much for giving me that piece of magic in my childhood, and to this day my wife, and I continue to make the tradition live on with our own children.

Anyway, by the time we celebrated New Years Eve, and awoke to 1967, we had once again enjoyed a wonderful family Christmas, which for me is the best event in my calendar. With the New Year comes an early concern for me, this year I will be eleven years old in April, that means after summer, I will no longer be going to primary school, but secondary modern school. I both look forward to it and worry about it, but I will not be going to big boy school for some time yet.

My friend Joes dad is taking me and Joe to St Ives today, although quiet this time of the year, it's still a great place to go. They have in my opinion one of the best Amusement Arcades in the whole of the West Country. When we arrive in St Ives, Joes dad parks the car, and we set off in the search of a fish and chip shop. Next we sit with our legs dangling over the harbour wall, while we eat our chips. After our lunch we walk through the little alley ways and head for the surfing beach, which is Porthmeor beach, a very popular surfing spot.

Then after playing on the beach we head off to visit the harbour, and by now the fisherman were landing their latest catch. We walked along the pier and watched them haul the boxes of fish up onto the harbour wall. This Always gets quite a crowd in the summer months, but today it was just us, and one elderly lady out with her dog. We then asked Joes dad, if we could also go and play on Porthminster beach, which is another one of St Ives great beaches, and also well popular with holiday makers.

Most holiday makers come to St Ives by train, using the branch line a beautiful scenic costal railway line. You catch this train from St Erth station, from here the line twists and turns along the coastline, calling at Lelant, and Carbis Bay on the way. I can think of no better way to take a trip to St Ives. St Ives is the home of quite a few famous artists and sculptors, such as, Henry Moore, Turner, Whistler, Dame Barbara Hepworth, Virginia Woolf, and Bernard Leach.

One of the most prominent landmarks of St Ives is the Island, which oversees Porthmeor beach, this landmark was once a promontory fort, of which it is thought, that it once had a protective ditch and rampart. I learnt at school that the old name for it, was Pendinas, with Pend-inas meaning fortified headland. It's an awe-inspiring place, and there is a chapel in addition to it. The chapel is at the top of the hill, it is St Nicholas Chapel built originally in the 15th century, and then rebuilt again I think in 1911. Now its Time to go back to the car, it's quite late by the time I get back home, so I had my supper and then went to bed early, quite tired.

With about a week left of my Christmas break from school, sad news today that Pete will be going away and Ann will not be far behind him. Because they work away from home, it always makes me feel so very unhappy when they have to leave. I never quite know either, when they will be back with us all again, so that makes it a little harder for me. I still have Christine to look after and to play with, but sure enough Pete and Ann soon leave. Now it is Christine and myself once again playing together with out them. I will try not to be too sad though, I know that Pete and Ann will be back, and we will be together again sometime. We continue to play with our new toys right up to the day before going back to school. Now in my bed, my thoughts turn to school tomorrow, and my friends, I think of Ann and Pete, and fall asleep.

CHAPTER FIVE

11 - Plus Looming

On return to school, the exam which will qualify British schoolchildren for grammar school, is one of the main topics the teachers talk about. Many people thought it was not a great way of testing children at that time. Of course, I knew nothing of this being around 10 years and 8 months old. However, now having read a lot of what people have said about the 11 - plus exam, I do not from my standpoint feel that it was the correct selection process. Nevertheless, of course neither my parents, nor me could have done any thing about that at the time.

This is my last year at primary school, and with the 11 - plus coming at some stage, homework as started to be increased. I recollect now, that this was the first signs of pressure from being at school, because up until then school had been a fun place to be. Now the realisation dawns on me of what is ahead, soon I will be going to big school. What would it be like? I thought to myself, I must admit the prospect of big school was a big worry back then. I do not know why, but the closer I got to September the more the fear grew. I can remember asking one of my teachers what failing the 11 - plus meant?, and he said that it would mean I would be not going to grammar school. Furthermore, he made the alternative sound some what menacing. As a result, I guess from an early age failure to me was made to sound very undesirable.

Now back in school I was finding local history lessons very interesting, I can recall studying about Geevor tin mine, which is found on the outskirts of Pendeen near St Just. Tin and copper have both been mined there and the more general area from at least the 1700s. Some of my friends dads actually work there now, and I know it must be very hard work. After the second Boer war, many Cornish miner's came back from South Africa, and carried out a lot of prospecting there. At the time of my schooling in 1967 there were 200 or more staff working at the mine, later much later in 1985, the bottom fell right out of the tin market. The mine struggled on a few more years until 1991, and then sadly it was closed down. Today Geevor tin mine, is a tin mining museum/heritage centre and many visitors pass through her doors each year.

I told my mum on return from school about the miners of Geevor, and she told me that in the old days the miner's wives made pasties for the miners, and that they made the pasties in a unique way. The pasties at one end were made of meat, potatoes, turnip and onions, but near the middle, a line, made from pastry divided the pasty in half. This was so the other half could have a sweet filling for the miner's dessert. Dad told me about the miner's lamp that Humphry Davy invented, and told me that Humphry Davy was born in Cornwall in 1778, and that around 1815, he invented the Davy lamp.

Davy made the lamp, in response to the danger miners faced from the methane gas and firedamp. You see, the naked flame lights, that were used by the miners to see while mining, ignited the gas and gave rise to many fatalities. Davy's lamp guarded the flame with gauze, this helped, however, it gave out less light, and rusting of the gauze produced while working in damp conditions, soon made the lamp less safe. One can only speculate, on what the conditions were like for these hard working men all those years ago.

After mum and dad had finished talking to me about mining, I stayed in the kitchen and watched mum making Cornish pasties, I frequently did this in my childhood, I found it so interesting. Moreover, it was this introduction into cooking which led me later on in the 1970s, to be competent enough to hold a position in the famous Lobster Pot hotel. The lobster Pot Hotel Mousehole, it's such an impressive place, the originating place of my catering career that's a few years away from starting yet.

I sit and watch mum intensely, first the pastry making and then vegetable preparation, next and lastly dicing the meat. I follow her every move, now the pasties are on the baking tray and the tops are covered with egg wash, then into the cooker they go. Soon I think to myself, the kitchen will have that aroma that all Cornish people love so much, the aroma of freshly baked Cornish pasties. We had pasties nearly every couple of days, I would have gladly eaten one every day if put in front of me.

Close, to the back of this book I have reproduced the recipe my mother used to make Cornish pasties, I use it, myself to this day now 42 years later. After my mum finishes cleaning the kitchen, I go outside and help her get the washing off the clothesline. Then play with Tibby while I wait for our evening meal of pasties, and meal time can't come soon enough for me. Tibby loves to eat the meat out of my pasty, he likes a bit of potato as well. He relentlessly hassles me for more and more, if I give in, he would eat more of it than me.

Later, after eating my pasty my thoughts turn to this weekend because on Saturday dad will be taking Christine and me to the Savoy cinema. This Cinema, is located about half way up Causeway head in Penzance, and is always good fun when ever we go. We use to go to the cinema most weeks, Christine, and I love going there, we buy sweets on the way, and it is the best way to spend Saturday mornings. We both looked forward to watching Donald Duck cartoons and the lone ranger this coming Saturday on the big screen. But for now my friends have come to my home to play with me, in the garden.

My friends and myself, all go out in the backfield to play, and I suggest we make up some bows and arrows. So next, we all set about making bows and arrows from some of the string and wood, that my dad had given us from his shed. We Spend the rest of the early evening until it's almost dark, running around after each other playing cowboys and Indians. Until its time for all my friend's to return home, I wave goodbye to them all and go inside and play with Christine with her toys.

Tomorrow is Friday already, so the weekend is well nigh here again, and I can't wait for my trip to the cinema. One of my friends, David lives in Alverton estate just up the hill from our cottage, I am having tea at his house this Saturday after the cinema. Therefore, I will be able to play on David's go-cart when I get to his house. He has a super homemade go-cart, that we have a lot of fun with, and Dad said when he has some time spare he will make me one, I can't wait. Anyway, now a nice bath, and it's off to bed, it's back to school tomorrow, but it will soon be Saturday.

Today and among other subjects, we learnt about world war two, and later in the afternoon I had music lesson's, I love music. My brother can play the guitar, and I hope to learn to play guitar myself one day, Petes started to learn me a bit. During today's music class, I learnt to play the bongo drums and the triangle, music lessons are a favourite of mine, I also have art this afternoon, and maths to finish with. There are so many musical instruments that our school has, I am learning to play as many as I can.

When I got home, I worked hard on my home work and later played with Tibby, and Christine, and spent some time talking to dad about world war two. Dad told me that during the war, he was a sailor and had served on a minesweeper, and that he spent is days sweeping the coast. He explained to me how he searched for unexploded mines that had drifted into our waters. Dad told me that thousands of unexploded mines had been placed in the sea, under the orders of Hitler. Furthermore, that he found many mines while serving on the ship he was on, he told me that most of the mines he looked for, were found floating in the English Channel.

Today is finally Saturday, and I am about to go to Penzance, to the Savoy cinema with Christine, been waiting for this all week. It's so much fun, to see all our favourites, all of course on a huge screen, I love daffy duck, Donald duck, goofy, and all those cartoon characters. Half way through the show a woman came around with tubs of ice cream, pop corn and sweets. I can remember the noise that children made, stamping their feet in excitement to the action films we watched. It was quite deafening, when everyone started to shout at the good or bad guy on the screen. At times you were hard pushed to hear any of the dialogue, and sat there reduced to lip reading almost.

The Savoy cinema claims to be the oldest cinema in England, and it was purpose built in 1912, and on many occasions the queues of children, reach quite a long way up Causeway Head, but its well worth the wait. When the show ends my friend David meets me outside, and my dad takes Christine home. David's dad takes me back to my friend's house in Alverton, which is not very far from my home. Next David takes me to a shed, and inside, there is a brilliant go-cart that his dad had made him. We take it outside and with it being a two-seat cart, both of us are soon zooming down the road to the sweet shop.

We park up outside the sweet shop, and I buy some fizzy flying saucers, and a pack of bubble gum, our pockets are now crammed full with sweets. We now set off towards love lane, and play for some time, going up and down the more hilly parts of the area there. Next we take the go-cart all the way back up towards the Rope Walk.

It is such a big hill, so when reaching the top of it, we rest and take a gulp or two of air by the AA phone box.

In the 1960s the AA use to wave to their members, I quite frequently saw an AA motorbike and sidecar going by. The rider would wave or give a salute, to all vehicles that carried the AA badge on their front bumpers. Now having had a good rest, we climb Back into the cart and off with the brake, and we were flying down the hill again. Half way down, we take a corner to quickly and all but ended up in the road. My sweets half scattered across the pavement, no damage done to us, so we just laughed about it, however, I now had a rather big hole in my trousers for mum to fix again.

Now at the bottom of the hill again, we sit outside the sweet shop and share a bottle of pop, Next we find a flat spot to play marbles on, I had a big bag of marbles, and my top ones were my huge alleys. An alley would be worth a particular amount of points so to speak, more than plain old marbles. During that game I can recall losing my special coloured alley, it was a particularly sad loss for me, because I had managed to get that alley to a points value of six.

With our marble game over, and now back at Davids house, its now time to go home, David's dad drives me the brief distance to the cottage, and I thank him. Then I go in and tell mum and dad what a great Saturday, I had, Nevertheless, I left out the bit about our go-cart crash of course, and told mum I had fallen over and had ripped my trousers. Anyway, my favourite programs on tonight, Dr Who it was well scary, don't laugh!, it was scary back in 1967, there wasn't that much to watch on the television back then. Later I hear Tibby meowing at the back door, I go to investigate only to find him with a mouse in his mouth, yet again, looking proud. I get mum to sort it out, and mum says to Tibby, "Tibby leave some mice out there, poor things!". Tibby had become a fine hunter, you would not think it to look at him, because you would more often than not, find him sleeping in the garden while sunbathing.

Looking back on those days, days of innocence, and fun, living in the country, With my family and Tibby, I knew even at ten years old, that life was good, and I feel that the cottage, woods, and a little cat, all played a magic part of my childhood. Dad and mum worked so hard, Mum had been with the woman's land army based in Gulval during the war, and the work mum did with the land army was worthwhile to her later. Mum, spent a lot of her working life working on the land, picking Cornish daffodils and anemones, which her land army days in the past had made her strong enough to do. Both my parents worked very hard for us, and I thank them for doing so, it would have been hard work for them back then.

A different matter that I notice when looking back is, we had a lot more home made meals, frozen food was not in abundance then, I certainly feel I turned out all the better for it, and slimmer. We had a full Sunday roast every weekend, and eat a lot of fruit and vegetables, and spent only a minimal amount of time watching the television. Furthermore, In my opinion, crime was much less then, also under age smoking, and drinking of alcohol, among teenagers was very low. Street crimes and stabbing you hardly ever heard of, my Mum and Dad, hardly ever locked our front door.

Peter and Ann when home made my life complete, between the two of them, they brought a different kind of magic. The magic of a big brother whom I looked up to, he was and still is a hero to me. Ann, so softly spoken and fair complexion and a great sense of humour, always helping me with things, whenever she was home. Finally, Christine, I spent more time with her of course due to our age. I always thought of myself as big brother in Pete's absence, and I took care of Christine in my own little way. Christine and me have a big bond, because we grew up together playing mostly together on our own, in the absence of our older brother and sister.

CHAPTER SIX

Aircraft and Legends

Today is Sunday, and I am going to Joes house to play for the whole day, and maybe go out some where in Joes dads car. His home is very near Porthcurno, a place I have learnt about in one of the encyclopaedias I had for Christmas. Porthcurno is naturally very famous regarding Telegraph cables, the cables run for miles under the sea, to many international destinations. It was way back in 1870 when the first of the Cables came up on to the shore of Porthcurno. Furthermore, they stretched all the way to India, later in 1872 the ETC the Eastern Telegraph Company Limited took over the cables.

When I arrive at Joes home, he wastes no time in telling me that later we are going to Lands End, I love the airport near there, I remember Pete had taken me once before. Moreover, I enjoyed watching the planes taking off the runway and then heading out off the cliffs. We played in Joes back garden until Joes dad called us, and soon we are on the way to lands End.

We park up near the airport, and soon spot the odd plane or two, I was told that the plane on the ground was a

Rapide, and also watch a pair of LET L13 gliders, glide by silently and gracefully unlike the powered planes. I know that if I was lucky enough to be able to fly, I would most definitely fly around the Longships lighthouse.

The Longships lighthouse, is just 1.25 miles out to sea from Lands End, staffed until recently, but now in 1967 is not manned any more. There are quite a lot of privately owned planes on the ground, and after a good long viewing of all the planes, we set off for lands End. Before long we needed to stop, to let a farmer with his dairy herd pass by, to enable him to get the cattle safe into the nearby field. It was so funny looking out the cars window watching the cows looking right back at me and Joe. This was and still is to this day, a very common sight around the country lanes and roads of Cornwall.

Now entering lands end, you sure do get a feeling of history, with the old Cornish name being 'Penn-an-Wlas', meaning end of the land. We stand by the famous sign just like thousands before us have, and the cold breeze laced with a slight hint of sea salt, can be detected. Gulls hover above effortlessly exploiting the stiff constant wind, as always searching for food. Furthermore, as we look over the edge of the cliff, I can see a small group of grey seals beached below, taking a break from the unrelenting rhythm of waves. In addition, it is so incredible to me, the amount of rabbits hopping around the area, they seem almost oblivious to people being near them.

Joe assembles his kite, and launches it up into the grey sky, and we share it for a while, meanwhile Joe's dad is busy taking pictures of the beautiful area surrounding us.

The kite makes a lot of noise as it struggles against the wind, so before long me and Joe agree to put the kite away, it's just too windy here today. I can see a ship a long way out on the horizon, and I think of a legend, the legend of the lost land of Lyonesse.

You see I like many have heard of this land, between Land's End and the Scillies, the land is lost under the sea. Folk tales tell of people hearing the bells of the lost city ringing, when the weather makes the sea rough. Furthermore, the legend says sailors have heard this bell, when during stormy nights they have sailed over the spot. I try to see if I can hear the bell ringing, but the wind muffles out all attempts. I think this is a great legend, and for a pair of young boys fills our imaginations, I love it here in lands End. Its also of course, famous for people who do the Lands End to John O'Groats, or of course vice versa. People over the years have done the trip in various ways, to many to mention. Most have done the End to End, as its known, for charity, others for the sake of saying they did it or to beat previous records.

It is so beautiful here, the cliffs and the sheer ruggedness of the place, all of which are steeped in history. Many people come down to holiday here, I feel so lucky that I live here, and that all this beautiful view is free for me. I check again to see if the seals are still below, but they have gone, probably they are hunting for fish. Its hard to believe how many people have stood by the world famous sign, to have their photo taken here in lands End. It's even harder to recall all the weird and wonderful ways people, have made the Lands end to John o'groats trip. For instance, I saw a man in a bath with wheels on, and a man who skipped the whole distance to name but a few, that have passed by our home. I see the seals reappear momentarily in the rough sea, and then under the waves they go once again.

I feel the threat of rain and hope it might be just a shower, but before long it is raining bucket loads, and it's back to the car. We wait but the bad weather looks set for the rest of the day, so with a passing glance towards the light-house I bid Lands End goodbye. However, I will be back some day soon, try stopping me. The roads are flooding on the way back to Joe's place, Joes dad thinks we might get major flooding if the rain keeps up. I have some food and a drink when we get back to Porthcurno, and then Joe's dad takes me home. The rain indeed caused a lot of flooding on the roads, and I think Joes dad for one, was well glad to get back home.

The rain is relentless, and I can say that when looking back, that the seasons were what you would have expected them to be in those days, I can recall many winters with snowfall, in comparison to today. My own children have suffered many years of disappointment, waiting for snowfall, but of course living in the far west of Cornwall, one would probably not expect that much in the first place. However, I can say that we did get a lot more in the way of snow, for sure during my early child-hood. A lot could be said about today's global warming crisis, when I look back at the weather we had back then, and compare with today's, things were different.

When I get back home, I hear dad talking about the recent news about the Vietnam War, I ask dad to tell me what it was all about. I must confess when I was a young boy, the news did not matter to me much, only some breaking news report got my attention. I did know that the conflict started around 1959, and I was just 3 years old then of course. Anyway, dad told me that war solves nothing, and that governments need to speak with each other more. Moreover, that innocent people are always hurt, I share the shame belief to this very day. I felt sad back then when hearing reports on the news about the Vietnam War, and listened to the news when ever I could. I hope that one day, governments all around the world, will communicate better with each other, and make wars a thing of the past. Sadly now aged 52 wars have raged without hardly a break in most parts of our world.

Its funny in a way looking back on my youth, at all the big names in pop music of the day, who are real legends now, and many are living ones. It may well have been because I was just 10 in 1966, but even though I lived through the swinging 60s, I feel like I completely missed it. Because I had so much more to do with my time, I hardly paid any attention to pop music. These days I hear my own children talking to each other or me, about groups or solo artists from my childhood!. In addition, they are telling me how cool this new group or artist is!!, I soon put them Straight of course.

My children often make me laugh these days, because even when I have told them that the song they are singing, is from my day, They reply "No Way not back in the dinosaur days!". Nevertheless, a lot of the big names back then, that I listened to, I only came to love by the time I reached about 17 years old. Therefore, I think it is quite strange how you can be oblivious to something as it happens so to speak, and then suddenly later on enjoy it.

My childhood in my opinion, was better by the lack of television programs and games consoles. We played board games more, read books more, and played outside more, and I am all the fitter for it. Looking at all the new hi tech equipment, I now have at my fingertips these days, it was far better back then when we had comparably less. I enjoyed playing with my younger sister, and simply reading a comic, or riding a bike was really great fun.

I find contentment with very little in the way of possessions, and back in my youth learnt, that you can get a lot from hardly anything, if you are just happy with yourself and others. At last the rain looks like stopping, if only it had when me and Joe were still at Lands End. Well before long the day had come to and end, and I was soon tucked up in bed with my comics, and my fond memories of this weekend.

The rest of January past through quite quickly and uneventfully, Pancake day, or shrove Tuesday if you prefer beckons once again. I will soon be laughing along with Christine, at dads attempts to flip over a pancake. A fun event for Christine and me, we never miss making pancakes on Pancake Day with mum and dad. Dad always of course, does the tossing of the pancakes, and I think he actually deliberately mess's up the throwing of them, to amuse Christine and me. Because one year the pancake ended up on his head, and stuck like glue, I wish I had a camera in my hand to capture that moment. This year, a pancake as fallen on the floor just under the kitchen table, I bend down to pick it up, and I find my toy pirate sword, and images of pirates rush into my head.

I can remember learning at school and from my brother Pete, and later from books, about pirates, buccaneers, and wreckers. Furthermore, that, around the 16th and 17th centuries, smugglers, wreckers, and pirates had quite a bit to do with the Cornish history. Reading Pirate's stories thrilled me as a young boy, and still does through blockbuster movies, at the cinema these days. Back when I was just a boy hearing all the stories of pirates and galleons, sailing just off the shores of Cornwall, was amazing. I enjoyed pretending to be a pirate with my plastic swords and black eye patch. I would race around the garden, with sword in hand not aware about what pirates really stood for.

I also love the folklore in Cornwall, whether it be about the Mermaid from Zennor story, or other stories, like the Cornish Piskies. Then there's the giants we have in the folklore in Cornwall, such as Cormoran, the giant of St Michaels Mount in Marazion, and Bolster the giant of St Agnes. I see Cornwall as a magical land of mystery, charm, and legends. It would take another whole book to describe what it means to me to be Cornish.

Anyway, great news for me, dad is going to make me a Go-cart, and I can help him make it. I go outside to his shed, and dad as 4 old pram wheels off Christine's old pram. He gives me a hammer and tells me to knock a nail or two into a plank, and then he placed a big bolt through it. Next, he makes a small box like encasement for my seat, Just the wheels now and fitting a handbrake. It's

finished!, I love it, it is the finest go-cart ever, I quickly
tow it around to the front of the cottage.

A rapid run to the top of the hill, and before long the go-
cart and me are whizzing towards the bottom of the hill
again, dads watching, and tells me to make sure, I stay on
the pavement. I hardly heard him, I must have ascended
that hill about a hundred times before I finally put my
new toy away for the day. That was a marvellous day,
helping dad to construct my own, my very own go-cart.
Tomorrow I will ask dad for some of his paint, and I will
paint my cart when I get some spare time. After tea mum
gives me the great news that Peter is coming home around
early March, and I start looking ahead to once again,
going hunting for the big one with him down the woods.

Today at school, as like every day is now becoming at
school, we continue to work hard on our fourth coming
11 plus examination. This is something I continue to
worry about, and it looms ever closer with every passing
month. I am getting progressively scared of what it will
be like to go to big school. This stems from I believe, the
fact that I have lived mainly in the country so far in my
life. Moreover, its fair comment to say, that up to now
that I have had very little contact, with children from big
towns or estates. I fear what a difference, and impact this
may have on me and my friends.

Apart from a few choice friends from Alverton, I have
perhaps some would say led a sheltered lifestyle, from say
the mainstream. Therefore, I worry privately not reveal-
ing it to my parents or Pete, and Ann. I hope that my anxi-
eties will be unsubstantiated in the end, but of course

I have nothing to judge it by, as I move ever closer to that day. Mum as begun to say I will be a big boy soon, and that I will be wearing long trousers and a jacket to my new school. This announcement in it self, is an endless reminder to me of the growing uneasiness, I feel each day.

I am pleased to get back home after school, to my new go-cart, and to get on with the job of painting it. I have some silver and red paint from dad to use, with Red being my favourite colour. I splash it on the main body of the cart, and use the silver for a few highlights. Now it is a stunner, I cannot wait to show David some time, Best thing is I will now be able to race his cart.

The remainder of February soon goes and Pete will be home today around teatime. Therefore, I will be running home from school tonight when I finish. The school day comes to an end, and I am like a bullet out of a gun, I run like the wind to get home to Pete. When I get home Peter is by the gate looking up the hill. I call out "Hi Pete", Pete says, "Mick, I got something for you here", and when I get to the gate Pete holds out a small package. I walk into our front garden, and open it, I can't believe my own eyes. Pete, had given me a brand new mouth organ, not any old mouth organ, but a chromatic one. This type has a button on the side to change the pitch of the notes, I will never forget it. The box had a picture of little Swiss chalets perched upon green mountains printed on it. In addition, inside was a piece of green felt that wrapped the mouth organ up.

I leapt up onto Pete and gave him an enormous kiss and a hug, I had always desired a mouth organ ever since

Peter had played one to me. He also played the guitar at the same time, using a special holder for the mouth organ. I must have sat for hours listening to my brother performing the songs of the day. I always thought the entire time that one day, I would play the mouth organ like Pete, and that day as come. I moved to the front room to practice and later to my bedroom, having driven mum mad with the noise I had been making. I blew my cheeks off every day, for days after, until I mastered it. Finally, I played a tune to Pete that I had rehearsed over and over again, I was so proud when he said I played well.

Tomorrow is the weekend again, and I will not be seeing Joe this weekend, because I want to spend time with Pete. I hope to go fishing down the woods, and try to catch that evasive large fish, the eternal big one. That fish seems to mess with us on every trip, I wonder if we will ever catch him. I think next time the big one is on the line, that I will just jump in the river and seize it, before it escapes our clutches again. I tell you, this fish should have been a cat, actually this fish has more lives than the humble cat. I hope we might get a little sunshine tomorrow, because it will bring the midges out, and fish always congregate around these places.

CHAPTER SEVEN

The Dawn of the Dark Sand

Plans of going fishing are soon neglected, after hearing the breaking news today, dad was listening to the radio, and the story of a huge tanker The Torrey Canyon had run into Pollard's Rock, located on the Seven Stones Reef. The Seven Stones Reef, is between mainland Cornwall, and the Isles of Scilly, and my brother knew it well.

Peter had many times been in the area of the accident, on account of the ships he had served on. As a result, we sat and listened into all of the reports, it was not long before we and every one else, realised that this was very bad. The tanker was nearing 1000 feet long I recall and was now breaking up, It had begun to leak thousands of tons of oil into the sea, which was the beginning of a massive environmental disaster. The radio broadcasts had stated that efforts had failed to float the tanker off the reef so far.

The tanker went aground around the 18th of March 1967, the next day a survey of the vessel was carried out. The news reports we listened to, reported that 14 of the ships cargo tanks out of around 18, had been completely holed. Attempts were made to try to float the massive oil tanker off the rocks using airbags and the tides. However, to no avail, the ship remained caught on the rocks, and other ideas were put into action. By the 27th of March stormy seas, had broken the ship in two, and the salvage operation was called off, next RAF planes were sent to blow the ship up with rockets and bombs.

When the news got out that the tanker was to be blown to bits, my brother took me down to a spot on the cliffs, where it would be possible to watch. It was so funny, because when we got to the point where it was possible to see the stricken tanker, a policeman told us to stop. However, Pete had other ideas, so we then went along the back of a path that ran parallel with the cliff top. From there we could see the planes making their bombing runs towards the oil tanker, we had to keep our heads down so as not to be seen.

The area was full of soldiers, police, and vehicles and around 40 or even more bombs were dropped on the tanker, and we saw it all happen, right in front of us. It was the most exciting thing I have ever seen in my life, I could hardly believe my own eyes, massive bomber planes flying above me. Then large black shapes falling out of them towards the stricken ship below, a loud bang as the first 1000 lb bomb explodes on impact.

You could see immense dense dark clouds of black smoke rising from the tanker, the smell was terrible, I can recall my eyes burning and watering for ages. The whole thing was right out of a Hollywood block buster, and being just 11 years old, the implications of all this, did not register in my mind. It was an adventure a real adventure, and

I had a front row seat to it. Bombers flying high all around me making runs towards the tankers, and seagulls making a hell of a racket, the vantage point we were in was filling up fast with new spectators.

I heard the shrill of a rocket being launched at the ship, we stayed there for ages watching all of this taking place, history in the making unfolding before my eyes. It will forever be imprinted in my memory, the sounds of bombs, and the smell in the air of smoke, you could have believed you were in a war. The ground beneath me shook with each new bombs impact on the ship below, a very sad day for Cornwall and Cornish wildlife.

When they dropped the napalm and petrol on to the wreck to help burn up the oil, a massive black swirling column of smoke came up. Not only had the planes dropped bombs, but rockets had also been fired at the tanker. The news reported that the bombs were a 1000 lbs each, and some had actually missed the wreck. I know One thing for sure, I had never seen anything like this in Cornwall, let alone anywhere else. It was just so unreal to be standing there, on a Cornish cliff top watching planes drop huge bombs on a stricken ship below.

The smoke was reported being seen a 100 miles away, It was exhilarating and quite frightening, massive explosions made the ground shake beneath your feet. To be standing there, watching bomb's huge bomb's being dropped on the ship below was breath taking. Eventually, the news broke that due to high spring tides, the fires that were hoped to burn up a lot of the oil were going out. Therefore, the bombing of the wreck was called off, what followed in the weeks and months to follow was just horrible.

Eventually, the super tanker broke up and her cargo belched out thousands of tons of oil, this produced a huge oil slick which in turn, was killing any creatures in the sea it came in contact with. Many foam booms were implemented to try and contain the slick, but this had limited success. This was our first major disaster of this magnitude, and very little was in place to combat it at that time.

The oil, was now affecting coastlines in France, not just our South coast or Cornish beaches, also reports of many thousands of sea birds, covered in oil dying on our beaches, or at sea. With beaches also being covered in thick oil, because the tanker had leaked tens of thousands of gallons of oil. Killing most if not all marine lives that it came across, it was a very sad time for all who witnessed it. The whole south coast of Britain was reported to have been affected, and the weather played a big part to.

In addition, I saw many American soldiers carried around in military trucks, who helped our army, also being deployed to clean the beaches. The Americans were drafted in from nearby military bases from around Cornwall. It looked like a war zone with all the troops, so many people were busy cleaning this mess up. Many beaches around Cornwall were being cleaned, by the council, troops, locals, you name it, Cornwall was World news due to this disaster.

I can remember watching countless dead sea birds washing up on the oil strewn beaches, and furthermore,

I looked for oiled birds myself, and gave them to people who were taking them to the sanctuary in Mousehole. I watched many people picking them up, and taking any living ones to the bird sanctuary. The bird sanctuary in Mousehole was inundated with thousands of oiled birds, and they cleaned them all, as did many other places.

Before long helicopters with large cargo nets attached, would be seen carrying large detergent filled drums, to any where an oil slick needed dispersing. Some areas where the oil was unreachable, below cliffs for instance, would have barrels of detergent discharged down to it, from above. Many hundreds of people and soldiers, could be found spraying detergent on to the oil, on beaches and out at sea, or where ever oil was found. Thousands of tons of detergent was used, and it is recorded that the detergent had a worse effect than the actual oil spill. This was due to the high toxicity of the components used in it. Over 40 vessels sprayed thousands of tons of detergent on to the floating oil at sea. Many people worked very hard indeed, to clear up this appalling accident, and one would hope lessons were learnt.

For ages after that, I remember many reports from around Cornwall and further afield, about the disaster and the damage it left. It was like a war zone, only difference was the wounded and dead were not human but wild life, although one man died attempting to salvage the ship, I believe. There are many stories about this disaster, but I write what I witnessed with my own eyes. It was a truly pitiful sight to behold an oil covered bird, but many birds were saved due to the hard work of a lot of people. I can recall that I walked down to Newlyn beach, to investigate the devastation, and was sad at what I came across. My rock pool was now beneath a thick cover of oil, with all that lived in it now dead, I wonder if ever again I will see creatures in these pools.

I can remember on a trip to Newlyn, while on the way down the Coombe, a convoy of military trucks passing me. I was on my toy scooter, one legging it down the road, on route to the beach. One of the soldiers in the back of the truck's waved to me, and I gave him a salute, and got one back from him. I of course tried to keep up with the truck, but it soon vanished into the distance. They would most likely be going to be deployed on a beach, to help with council and other workers to clean up the oil. On an arrival at most beaches, you would see people dressed in protective clothing striding through huge amounts of oil. Many with huge hoses that were belting out detergent, on to the oil on the beach. Others would be wiping up oil with paper type towels, what a messy job.

Around the 24th and 26th of March there was a South Westerly storm, and the winds brought the oil ashore. I can remember seeing Bulldozers and men working on the beach at Sennen, pouring detergent all over the beach. From where I stood, they appeared to be bulldozing it under the sand. I never did find out if the oil was really being bulldozed under the sand, but have read other accounts from people who wrote the same thing. I heard many reports from other towns, about how Cornwall was being hit bad in with regards to this oil, now washing up on our shores.

Amongst so many other places hit, was Gursney, it was hit bad to, with thousands of tons of oil hitting their beaches. The one thing I still ponder about is, where did all the oil, that was cleaned up off our beaches go?. You see, I can remember seeing rags, and paper towels being thrown down to soak up the oil. Furthermore, heaved into trucks, but have no notion where this waste ended up, and at the time, it seemed to be not that important. The poor birds, it hurt to see them struggling, covered in thick oil, so stressed and scared, fighting for their very existence. Box's of birds were taken to the sanctuary in Mousehole, where they would have the oil meticulously cleaned off.

Even years after this catastrophe, I can still remember sitting on the beach with mum and dad, getting our garments ruined with thick oil deposits, that could still be found all over the rocks. It mattered not where you rested, oil was all over the place, and was still coming in on every tide. The beaches we used were Newlyn beach, and the beaches in Wherry town, all of which still had lots of oil here and there. I could pick up stones and stick them together, by utilizing the oil upon them to construct a kind of oily rock sculpture.

It sure was a very bad time in history for Cornish people, and it was an appalling tragedy leaving its mark for years to come. Next, on the radio and television we hear that there as been a major foot and mouth disease outbreak in England. It's truly turning out to be quite a bleak year, this year. Looking back on it, with the reality that summer was just a few months away, it gave everyone an overwhelming sense of desperation. Especially, for the local authority to clean up in time for the 1967 tourist influx, that was just 3 months away. Therefore, I am not surprised at the enormous effort and clean up operation, I witnessed all those years ago. It would have been a very stressful time for all, and so many people worked hard to clean it all up.

We had quite a few lessons at school, regarding the oil spill in Cornwall, and listening to some of the other Children's accounts of the catastrophe was extremely interesting. The Torrey Canyon was the first super tanker to have an accident of this magnitude, and I hope it's the last. By the time the main story of the disaster had been played out, my brother Peter was back to sea again. Easter though is just around the corner, so perhaps we can fish for trout again down the woods.

I have been a bit silly today, Christine and me were out playing in the field at the back of our garden. I noticed an electric fence, so always being interested in adventure so to speak, I decided to carry out a test. I tried to trickle some spit from my mouth towards the pulsating electric wire. The idea was at the last moment to pull away before my spit hit the wire. Well, I got that one wrong, my whole mouth was met with the most agonizing pain, much to the entertainment of my sister Christine. Hope Christine forgets about it, mum would be angry with me.

Anyway, the pain was quite short lived, needless to say I would not be doing that again! In a hurry. I checked my pond at the top of the field, and thought to myself at least the oil spill had not killed my frogs. I could see mum as I squatted by the pond, she was placing the washing on the clothes line. The bed sheets bellowed in the wind, and then I watched dad come up the steps, with a cup of tea in his hands. He then beckoned to me to come to him, when I got to dad, he had a lucky bag for me. I loved lucky bags, as did Christine, a lucky bag would have some sweets, a toy maybe a book or crayons inside. There was a boy and girl version, so it was always fun to open up our bags to see what each other got.

My favourite toy out of a lucky bag was, a cap bomb, fundamentally a cap bomb looked like a little rocket. You would place a cap, an explosive cap, that you brought back then, for toy guns in the front of it. Then throw it up in the air, and when it hit the ground the cap would give off a really loud bang. Dad took mine off me for a short while, after I went upstairs, and dropped it out the window close by him. It frightened the life out of him, I broke into a hysterics but dad was fuming with me. Later on he saw the funny side though, and I managed to get my rocket bomb back.

Next week is the start of Easter so soon we will be eating lots of lovely chocolate, I always get at least 5 Easter eggs, and a special Easter present. In addition, a few weeks off school and the best thing I hope for, is that Ann and Peter will be home again. I will also get to watch mum make hot cross buns and Easter flaky pastry cakes. It's a great time of the year, we get Easter eggs off so many people, and I know before Easter even arrives, that I will end up eating to much.

CHAPTER EIGHT

Chicken in the Basket

Little did I know that one day, I would become a chef, from watching mum baking in the kitchen, that gave me an early insight into cooking. My mum was an exceptional cook and her food was delicious, it inspired me to develop into quite a good chef in my own right, later on in my life. Today mum is preparing to make our Easter cakes, my favourite must be the large flaky type Eccles cake's mum makes so well. She was so meticulous with her pastry making, never hurrying it, but manipulating it gently into the correct consistency.

For today, of course, my abilities only run as far as cutting the pastry into forms for mum, but it is great to be of help. Mum makes ready the stuffing, and I get to spoon it onto each pastry round, I have cut out. Now the best bit, I get to lick the spoon and eat the excess that is left in the bowl. Next, mum's concentration moves to making hot cross buns, sausage rolls, and saffron cake. Saffron cake is my very favourite cake, and it is a firm winner with us Cornish folk. Personally, I will eat as much as I can get, with Cornish butter spread all over it, pure ecstasy on a plate.

The aroma of newly baked saffron cake filled our cottage, it was a superb cake and one that my mum loved to make and eat. Mum loved to put a dollop of fresh Cornish clotted cream, on her slice of saffron cake. I can see us all now sitting around the kitchen table, with freshly made saffron cake, with heaps of Cornish butter spread on it. Back In those days my mum managed to purchase fresh saffron, in little sachets from the local baker in Newlyn, or maybe Penzance, I never did find out where.

My mum appeared to bake every other day, such was her love for fresh homemade cooking, mum also baked fresh bread from time to time, another wonderful aroma. It made every part of me want to eat, the moment the aroma presented under my nose. Mum made up what I use to call Chicken in the basket, a small wicker basket would be lined with cotton wool, and then small chocolate eggs would be placed within. In addition, in the mix would be little yellow cotton wool chicks, and one large chocolate egg.

Christine and myself would get one of these baskets each, and Easter egg's from Ann, Pete, Auntie Flo, and Uncle Alf. Some times, we had as many as six eggs each, and finished up quite sick towards the end of Easter. This once again was yet another magic celebration every year that like Christmas was brought to life by my parent's. My parents, although not religious in a big way, taught Christine and me about the real meaning of Christmas and Easter. However, like many children the magic and fun, sweets and presents were what we enjoyed the most.

My dad and mum were not rich, and never did get rich, but I know that my dad and mum worked very hard for us all. Most nights dad could be found besides the radio, checking his horse bets he had put on earlier, and on Saturdays checking the football results. He never bet to much bless him, but I know he always dreamt of being able to take mum, to some exotic place for a holiday one day. I can remember how excited he use to get, when listening to the results, and see the sadness come over his face when he had lost. My dads hobby was collecting postage stamps, he had quite a big collection of stamps, from all around the world, I use to love looking at them with him. He had at least 8 albums of stamps, and he would also sell some to other collectors.

Well, after consuming all of our Easter eggs, we all went for a walk down Newlyn Coombe, every Easter we would go for an Easter walk, really looked forward to it every year. We came out of our cottage, and turned right, walked along the road down to the crossroad's, a right turn would head you off towards St Just, straight on would eventually take you to lands End, but we would turn left. A slight hill leads to a little bridge across a river, not just any old river but the one Pete, and I fished. I stopped here and pulled dads hand, and told him all about the big one me and Pete fished here for. While standing here you can also just see The Stable Hobba fish meal factory through the trees.

Next the road turns to the left, and you have a small hill, at the top we carry on and after the road takes a slight turn to the right, to our left is the entrance to the Rubbish dump. This, is the dump where my dad and my brother

Peter go to, searching for any useful discarded items. Now we head down a hill for a while, and here you come across a big shed, within this shed you will find the horse and cart, that's used to deliver our vegetables to our cottage. I love this place, because you can hear the horse breathing through the slat's of wood, that the shed is made of.

I call out to him, knowing that he will recognise my voice, my dad tells me not to disturb the horse, but I continue anyway, because I know the horse loves me. He begins to acknowledge me by making a hell of a noise, so much so that dad tells me to stop again. I did stop at this point but Nevertheless, I knew the horse was saying hi to me, he always did, when we met. I could see his eye looking through a hole that was in the side of the shed. Anyway, it was time to go so I look forward to seeing him again when next he visits our home. Nearly arriving in Newlyn now, on my right are the crab merchants, and to my left St Peter's Church. We have reached Newlyn bridge, now over the top of it, and we join the large queue outside of Jelpert's ice cream shop.

I cannot remember a time when we have not had to queue, to buy this incredible ice cream, but the wait is well worth it. Inside the shop dad got a large tub each for Christine and me, with a flake in each. Mum always has her tub of ice cream topped off with fresh Cornish clotted cream. Then we walk to the Seaman's mission and sit on a bench nearby, we stop a while there, and dad spots Mr Jelpert and says hello. Mr Jelpert, was taking a batch of newly made ice cream, from his little dairy where he makes it do his shop. There was a small dairy just a little way up Paul hill, on the left hand side going up, and in there, Mr Jelpert made the ice cream everyday. Having now finished eating our ice cream, we walk towards the pier, the gulls are making a heck of a noise, so it is clear fish are being landed.

Further along and just before we get onto the pier, a group of old sailors are sitting, quietly reminiscing I think, maybe about when they sailed the seas, telling each other stories, while white smoke comes out of their pipes. One winks at me, and I give him a smile back, I guess they miss being young and sailing the seas. A little further on you can hear men singing Cornish sea shanties, the sound is coming from the Star pub. I suspect that many are taking a well deserved break from the sea, it is in my opinion the hardest job in the world, being a fisherman.

I take a look over the harbour wall, and a large fishing boat below is preparing to land a huge catch. The men below on the deck are busy filling up plastic trays with fish of all descriptions. Next, another fisherman sling's down a rope, and the trays of fish are attached, and then heaved up on to the quay. I move forward and look at them, and then a man puts all the trays onto a small truck, next I watch him drive away. I know where he is going, he is going to put the fish into cold storage until tomorrow, in Newlyn fish market, he will then cover the fish over with ice, that's made in the ice factory in Newlyn. Next, very early in the morning the market will once again fill up, and local businessmen will bid to buy the fish for restaurants, fish and chip shops, to name a few.

I have been to see this market operating, my friends dad work's in the fish market, and he took us both there once.

It was amazing, all the boxes of fish are lined up and then a large crowd of business people listen to the auctioneer. Then, they raise up their hand's in an attempt to win the tray of fish with the highest bid. If they win, a man will then place a piece of paper on the tray, bearing the winner's name. This happens early in the morning, and it is very interesting to see this part of the operation. So far I have seen the trawlers and boats go out, and then land a catch of fish. Furthermore, I have watched as they cover the fish in the trays with ice and then store them, then finally the fish are on sale in the fish market. I then enjoy eating fish and chips quite often thanks to the brave fishermen of Newlyn, these guy's go out in all weather condition's doing one of the worlds's most dangerous jobs.

From the corner of my eye, I see a trawler leaving the harbour, I can see two men on her deck, and they are moving buckets and nets about. I then run to the wall behind me, and can see the trawler now leaving the harbour behind. They may be going to fish many miles off land's End or perhaps off the coast of France. Very soon it has gone out of sight, and mum asks me would I like to go for a walk along the promenade, and I smile which suggested a yes. I can see that the rocks in the sea are exposed in Wherry town, so Chris and me are well excited, because we enjoy playing on those rock's. We have our buckets and spades along with us, and soon have much crab and shrimp's from the rock pools in them. Before long we set off along the path that runs besides Newlyn beach and past the tennis courts.

We arrive in Wherry Town and dad and mum sit on the beach, we go out to the rock's and look around for crab's.

The rock's still have oil on them in place's from the oil spill incident, so we need to be careful. Christine and I find quite a lot of crabs, and shrimps which we put back in the pool after careful examination. Now with our tummies hungry were off again, to get sweet's from the shop at the bottom of Alexandra Road. We then walk as far as the Bathing pool, and around battery rocks and take a walk across Penzance Harbour. We also walk to Penzance train station, I love looking at the trains, and I love the noise that the trains engine makes. Mum gets a cup of tea from the railway station cafe, and Christine and me have a glass of orange, and we sit for a while. Then it's back to home to have a good portion of mum's saffron cake after a very nice day.

On the way home we walk up the Abbey slip steps, that leads to Chapel Street. On the way up Chapel Street, we go by the Admiral Benbow public house, dad tells me that this pub has a secret passage towards the back. The passage was used to smuggle goods up from the Harbour in days of long ago. In addition, he told me that Chaple Street was the oldest street in Penzance. I learnt at school that the Admiral Benbow use to be a place, the Benbow pirates liked to come to.

The pub it self, was built around the 17th century, and is actually mentioned in the book Treasure island. I love the figure on the roof pointing a gun, dad said it is supposed to be a young man, who went up on the roof to distract the Revenue men. However, it went wrong and he was shot and fell off the roof. I love this place, I have always loved the many stories about Cornwall's pirate history, and this place has quite a history. It's probably no surprise to readers that I enjoy stories of pirates, and with me living in Cornwall, I have heard many.

We carry on to the bus stop and soon my leg's can rest, unlike lucky Christine, she's been on dad's back for the last hour or so. We arrived at the bus stop, and in very little time are soon on a bus. Soon I can get my belly filled up, I am starving, I will be sure to dream of pirates tonight. When I got home, I took out my pirate gun and sword, and lay myself out on the settee, I pointed my gun at dad like the figure on the roof of the Benbow. Dad, then takes my sword and beckons me to attack him. Therefore, I let him have both barrels of my gun, dad pretends to die slowly while I am pretending to re-load my gun.

Mum call's us to the dining table, and Christine and myself are given a very large plate of food, consisting of sausage rolls, saffron cake and luncheon meat sand-wiches, all to be washed down with lemonade. Then after-wards we sit contented watching the television, we only had a black and white television in those days. Some times when we were allowed to stay up late, we would watch the television until it ended. When I was growing up, when the programs came to an end for the night, god save the queen was transmitted on the television. Shortly after that, a very loud beeping sound would be transmitted, and would only go away when you turned your Tv Set off. The funny thing was, that when you had turned the Tv set off, a white spot in the middle of the screen, would take ages to disappear. Its been another great family day out, and we give mum and dad a very big kiss each, and with that its time for bed.

With Easter now over and the new School term about to start, I am now of course in the last year of primary schooling. Moreover, after the summer holidays If I fail the 11 plus exam, I will be going to secondary modern school. Trouble is I do not wish to go to grammar school in any case, because most of my friends will in all probabilities, end up in a state school. Either way it's a nerve-racking time for me, and it eats away at me day by day, I really hate the fact I will soon leave this school I love. I am so scared by now you see, I have heard many stories from my friends older brothers and sisters concerning secondary modern school. Furthermore, I really worry about what I hear on a daily basis, I worry about the bullying, that my friends older brothers and sisters are contently talking about, most of my friends are really scared.

I did try to approach mum about it a while ago, but I got half way through saying I was getting worried, about going to big school and mum just told me not to worry. I did not push the fact that it had been a major concern for me this last year, I wish I did because It may well of benefited me. I really hope though that all my best friends will be coming along with me, it would be an unimaginable situation, if I ended up in a new school with out any of my mates.

CHAPTER NINE

The Summer of Change

The sun radiates down on me and Pete this afternoon in late May, we have just started to pack up our fishing gear after a satisfying fishing trip to the woods. We managed to catch two rainbow trout, and one brown one, which soon will be cleaned and, in mums fridge. We are debating our catch when we hear dad shouting at the top of his voice, "Michael, Peter, dinner is ready" echoes through the woods, dad would always call out to us that dinner was ready. We would shout back that we were on our way home, you could clearly see dad standing at the top of the lane, with his hands cupped over his mouth. It would take us at most 10 - 15 minutes, depending on where we were in the woods to get back home. We have pasties tonight for our tea, and while sitting at the dinner table, mum told me I could go to the Bathing pool tomorrow.

Being late May the Penzance bathing pool is now open, and I once again spend a day there, it opens around the 11th of May most years. I find it easy to memorise the first opening day in May, primarily because the 11th of May is Christine's birthday. I take enjoyment in going to the pool to swim, I could go every day because it's always so much fun. When ever I go to the pool, dad gives me some money to buy sweets, and a drink of which I always spend in the bathing pool Cafe.

I love the cafe there, my friends, and I frequently go in there, to buy our sweets when at the pool. Then we get changed into our swimming costumes in one of the little changing huts provided. We spend a lot of our day playing at being human bombs, we jump from the wall into the pool, and when flying in the air you curl your body in a special way, and then lean back. Therefore, when you enter the pool the shape of our bodies, causes an enormous amount of water to rise up into the air. This causes a huge splash onto Any unfortunate person who happens to be trying to get into the water at that moment.

The bathing pool as a spring board and a high diving board, I am ok on the spring board, but will need more time to build my confidence up to attempt the much higher one. It's a great place to go to, and after swimming you can just lay down and sun bath around the sides of the pool. The concrete gets well hot from the heat of the sun, and lying on a towel is well advisable. My mates and I are always being told off by the lifeguards for splashing people with our bombs.

We get told off mostly for bombing someone who is yet to get into the pool, when we see a person at the bottom of the steps, testing the water with a little toe, we bomb the area and get them soaked. Next we swim off quick of course, but we always end up being chased around the pool by the lifeguard. However, we find it quite easy most times to keep one step ahead of him.

One particular lifeguard spends a lot of his time telling my friends and me off, we can hardly move an inch without him in our face. Understandably though, he is just doing his job, and we are just being little rogues. A different issue we did that displeased the powers to be in the bathing pool, was to jump or dive off the wall into the sea. Many of my friends were banned for weeks from being able to come into the pool, or even an entire summer season. I use to jump off the wall myself, but never got seen thankfully, I was a just a little more careful.

I spent whole days at the bathing pool, I would urge you to pay a visit the next time you're in Penzance, it's a lovely place to spend a day with friends or family. The summer of 1967 was a peculiar one, during trips to the beach with mum and dad, I can remember swimming and then seeing tiny slicks of oil moving towards me and the beach. This was from the Super oil tanker that had met its end on the seven stones reef earlier in March, and its still refreshing one's memory of the incident from time to time. In the 1960s we had to keep clear of raw sewage that was float-ing around, so oil in addition to this was just aggravating an already bad situation. In those days there was a pipe that terminated just off Newlyn beach, it was a sewage pipe, and raw sewage was often something that greeted you when swimming.

It depended which way the tide was flowing with regards to both the oil or the sewage back in 1967. We just desired to play in the sea, but the oil was a problem that summer as I wrote before. Oil, still covered a great deal of stones and bigger rocks, it was very hard not to get it on your-self, and with each new tide, came the risk of new oil, you never really knew from one day to the next, if any oil was about. Christine and me would make sand castles, and oil was actually in the sand in many parts of the beach.

We would sit on the beach eating our sandwiches, and sharing a large bottle of lemonade. I would make huge sand castles for Christine and of course bury her in the sand. The oil would be on our feet and arms, I found your feet always picked up most of the oil, especially the sides of your feet. All around us would be many seagulls competing for our scraps of food, that we had not consumed.

The one thing that was so different back then, was our money, the penny for example, a huge coin, and you got 240 of them to one pound!!. We had shillings, a shilling was worth 12 pennies, 20 shillings to a pound, and the three-penny bit, you got 4 to a shilling. A ten shilling note was worth 120 pennies, two ten shilling notes were worth one pound. In addition, I also remember a half crown, that being worth 30 pennies.

I will not write about all of the types of money, we had in my youth but when we went decimal around 1971, the pound was reduced to just 100 pennies. Furthermore, a lot of the older generation had a very hard time coming to terms with the new money. No wonder people were confused, the pound lost 140 pennies, most people I knew called it a complete rip off. I knew quite a lot of my mums friends, and they had a dreadful time learning the new currency.

Decimalisation was not in my opinion, excepted with open arms when it did come on the scene in 1971. Of course it had been talked about a lot in the 1960s, but when it eventually became the new currency, I for one definitely missed our old money. Mind you, having just written that looking back on my mum, sowing up my holed pockets in my trousers, I bet she was glad the larger of the coins went. The pennies in particular were so big, and you had so many of them to carry around. My trouser pockets always needed patching up by mum, and being young I had more pennies than pounds.

Every thing was different back then, police used among other things that I can remember, the Ford Anglia and the Austin Cambridge. The AA, the vehicle breakdown service, drove around not just on motor bikes but in brightly coloured yellow mini vans. And, with regards to a great British tradition, I could read an interesting passage of maybe older news, while consuming my fish and chips. Because back in 1967 our fish and chips were served up on some greaseproof paper, and then wrapped in old newspaper.

Oh, and not to forget our other iconic English landmarks, the telephone kiosks. Back then one would go into the kiosk and after fumbling around for change, put some money in the coin box. Next, you would dial the number, if you got an answer you would push the button marked (A) to release the money to pay for the call, if there was no answer you would instead press button (B) and your coins would be returned.

Well, anyway On the way back home from the beach, mum and dad would put Christine on one of the lion statues. Christine loved sitting on them, the bronze Lions are just across from the promenade. In addition, we would some times be taken for a walk through the beautiful sub tropical Morrab Gardens. Which, close to the top end of the gardens you will come across an outstanding water fountain. It is complete with an ornate seal, balancing a ball and a fish spouting out water.

Morrab gardens, water fountain was a fond favourite for both young and old alike, Christine and me splashed each other with water, while playing by it. You will come across a memorial to the Boer war, and a bandstand, it's truly a lovely garden and just a few minutes from the town centre. We also walked often past the towns library, that's situated towards the top of Morrab Road. My dad always sits me upon an old Spanish cannon there, that came from the Spanish Armada fleet, every time we walk by, I must sit on it.

Well today is the first day of the summer holidays, I have failed my 11 plus and so did a great deal of my friends. As a result after the summer holidays I will be off to Secondary modern School, I am very worried about this. The good news is nine of my very best friends will be starting at the new school with me. That makes it a little better in my mind, but I remain apprehensive to say the least. I am in no ways a weak child, and I think I am more than capable of sticking up for myself, but I detest violence. Never mind for now, Peters still home and we are going to Porthcurno beach today. Porthcurno has a superb sandy beach and is well popular, and one of my favourite seashores in Cornwall.

Porthcurno beach is nestled between steep cliffs each side, and you will find quite a lot of beautiful shells here. Not so far from here is the very well known Minack Theatre, a wonderful open air theatre. The theatre is actually built on the Cornish cliffs, and is a well known landmark to many. Porthcurno is Renowned also for the transatlantic telegraph cable, that I have already written about previously. The rise and fall of the tide here, to my mind makes it yet another great place at times for belly boarding or surfing. I really enjoy searching for shells on this beach, and Pete always talks of gold coins that may have washed up, from some nearby sunken treasure chest.

Pete and me explore the beach a little more, and we come across a cave and start to investigate the inside. It was damp and dark inside and the feint drip of water, could be heard, dripping through the hard granite stone above. The further we went into the cave, the more the inside temperature dropped. You could almost feel like you were a smuggler of long ago, who had landed upon this beach. Maybe a sailor, or even a pirate sought sanctuary from the bad weather in this very cave. My mind raced, we looked in every nook and cranny, hoping to find the odd gold coin or treasure chest, nothing was found of course, however, it was an incredible rush and great fun for me.

We could only go in so far though, because the main passageway to the inside of the cave, had been blocked. The passageway had got blocked due to the past tides, that over the years had brought in bits of wood and old rope. Eventually, we turned back and it was a good feeling to get out. Pete and me talked for some time about the pirates of long ago, and smugglers, which made me think about what went on around the coast long ago. I had already learnt at school that wreckers had used the light from their lanterns, in hope to lure the unsuspecting ships to the rocks or shallow water.

Now, with the unsuspecting vessel wrecked far below on the rocks, the wreckers would go down, and collect the cargo that had been onboard. Alternatively, on a stormy night when many ships sank legitimately, due to very bad weather, they would go and collect that washed up cargo. Rum, and tobacco to name but just a few treasures, would be the nights catch so to speak.

I look at our beautiful rugged coastline, the coves and sleepy villages, towns, and country side, and I am inspired by its mysteries, and legends. I am confident that any visitor to Cornwall, will also be surprised by the mix of beauty, legend, and stimulating tales and folklore. A week in Cornwall will last in your memory a lifetime, Cornwall delivers something for everyone. What ever turns you on Cornwall has it, so if you're a surfer, you have to name but a few, Sennen near Lands End, or Porthmere beach St Ives.

Alternatively, of course just a bit further around the coast from St Ives, you have the spectacular surf that you will find in Newquay. If you like walking, our coastal walks are magnificent, and food lovers will be impressed by our immense range of restaurants. That among other dishes, prepared, include freshly caught fish from our own costal waters daily. What ever it is you come to Cornwall for, you will be greeted with a warm friendly welcome, from all of the Cornish people.

Anyway, after a great day out in Porthcurno, we head back to home, but we stop to take a look around Drift dam. Drift, is a place Pete had been telling me about, it's just outside of Sancreed. Pete says it is an exceptional place to fish for trout, and that he will pay for a fishing session there one day. On arrival home, I tell mum all about the cave, and then I play with Tibby before our evening meal. A bit later I practice playing my mouth organ and kazoo. Before I went to sleep that night, mum came into my room and told me that she wants to measure me up tomorrow for my new school uniform. And, That we will be going shopping for my new clothes for school later this week. I ask mum if we could go to the beach again tomorrow some time, and she said maybe.

Chapter Ten

Penzance Shopping Spree

The next day mum asks me to come into the living room, then puts a tape measure against my body, and starts noting measurements for my new school uniform. Once again, my mind wakes up to the fact, that its nearly time to go to my new school, and apprehension rushes over me. The stories I have overheard from older boys who go to the same school, would trouble any body, I fear the worst while recalling what I had heard. The images I see in my imagination of a new school, make me fidget and mums tell me to stay still.

Dad came in, his body was covered in sweat, he had been cutting the grass to the sides of the drive that leads up to the manor house. He can see mums occupied measuring me up, so makes a cup of tea for mum and himself. Then he goes out to the garden, and commences sharpening his shears with a large sharpening stone. After mum finishes measuring me, Christine and me gather up our buckets and spades for the beach, and also my new diving mask and snorkel.

We assist mum in the preparation of sandwiches and drinks, next we say goodbye to dad, and we set off for

Newlyn beach. We of course have a lovely day on the beach, made all the better seeing as Ann joined us, she had come home from Truro for a few days. Ann was a nurse, and worked at Truro hospital, its great that she's home again, I miss her so much.

We go to Truro city quite a lot, it's a great place to shop in, and one of my favourite walks will be found there. This walk will take you about a mile along the river, to the village of Malpas, there the Truro river meets up with the river Tresillian. Next the river twists and turns towards Falmouth, its so beautiful out along this stretch of river. I think Ann is so cool being able to live in the city, I will miss her when she goes back to work in the hospital. I wish both Pete and Ann lived with me and Christine all the time, It would be so very perfect then. Nevertheless, I understand they need to work, and more importantly I guess they need their own space. It's just so much fun when we are all together though, I always miss them both so much.

Well, this summer is moving quite fast, and it will soon be Big fair day, but for now me and mum are in Penzance shopping for my new school uniform. We enter a shop, and before long I am trying on various trousers, blazers and a few ties, and finally 3 shirts. Eventually, mum is happy, and we then embark on a tour of many shoe shops seeking a pair of black shoes. After shopping, we then searched for a snack bar, and have a cup of tea and a pasty each. After a swift lunch were off shopping again, this time for pens and pencils, rulers, writing books. Finally, we get the bus home, and I am subjected to a fashion show of my new uniform in front of everyone. I don't like the tie, its way too hot to wear, but I guess I will have to get use to it fast.

After changing back into my play clothes, and now feeling more comfortable, I go out to the back garden to play with Tibby. I felt really sad, sad that I would soon be leaving a school that I loved. A few of my friends would be going to grammar school, and I would miss them for sure. Nevertheless, it was a reality now, so even though my heart was heavy, I knew it had to be. I gave Tibby a real big cuddle, and then took him inside and gave him a big bowl of milk. What a good friend my cat Tibby is to me, I love this bundle of fur so much. When ever I come home from anywhere, Tibby runs to greet me, with out fail.

It's my mums birthday today, and the 3rd of June also heralds the Corpus Christi fair, this huge fair is held each year in Penzance at the recreation ground. It's the largest fair we have in Cornwall, and my very favourite one. It's a giant of a fair, Dad and mum will be taking Christine and me up to the fair tonight, I really hope the weather stays fine like it is now. Now readers, I was back then fair mad, could not get enough, so I cannot wait for tonight to come.

Well, the weather held, it's a lovely sunny evening, and we catch the bus to Penzance, and then walk up to the recreation ground. I will endeavour to give you a guided tour of what it was like for me to go to this fair. The road leading up to the fair ground would be full of market traders. Both sides of the pavements were crammed with everything you can think of. When we approached the entrance dad would buy us a toffee apple or candy floss, and then we would embark on a walk around the fairground first.

This fair would have at least 4 lots of dodgems, two big wheels, an octopus ride, two or more Noah's arks, two twister rides, dive bomber, ghost train. In addition, an array of side shows, of which I will describe later, and of course children's rides. The best part was, it came and still does every year, and it was one of the main things I saved my pocket money for. I can always remember having at least 10 shillings I had saved, plus dad would also buy me sweets and extra rides.

My favourite side show was the boxing booth, boxers that worked for the fair would stand up on a stage. While a Mc would ask challengers to come up to fight them. If you lasted, I think three rounds, you would get paid an amount of money. A person before long would volunteer, and we would all pay to go in and watch the fight. What fights, they were, I felt sorry for most of the challengers, although some did actually win. It was so exciting though, I can remember seeing old ladies hitting the fighters with umbrellas, and hearing excited people screaming above the noise at the boxers.

Then of course we had the freak show, I can remember one year the 6 legged sheep, what a site that was, my dad took an age to stop laughing over it. Mum would be sat down playing bingo for prizes, dad would love the darts, and me, I loved the tin men rifle range. I always managed to shoot them all down, and unfailingly got either a cat or dog made out of plaster of Paris, no surprise there.

Then Christines and mine favourite of all time, the gift elephant, dad would put a coin in this machine, and press boy, or girl, then this little grey elephant would move into a cave. After a little while, it came back out the other side, and it would drop off your prize. The prize would be in a suitably coloured box, and will always be for me, the best part of going to the fair.

Dad took me on the dodgems, and mum would take Christine on the Golden gallopers, a ride with lots of wooden horses on. We would have quite a lot of rides, and of course a hotdog each, we were truly spoilt at the fair. Finally on the way out, mum and dad would look at the market stalls, and would probably buy new Towels and sheets. This event held each year, was among one of my most favourites from my childhood.

The next day I go to up to Alverton Estate to play with my mates, we sit and talk about our new school. It becomes apparent that we have all overheard the stories, and that we are all scared. We decide right there and then, that we would be there for each other, in the new school no matter what. The next thing we did was to go and play in the woods at the back of Alverton, called Blue Bell Dell. We Spent a lot of time up trees, and sliding down the earthy slopes towards the bottom of the hill there. We had great fun, and of course it was right near to the rubbish dump, and to the woods by my home.

I smile when I think of the time my friend found an old tin bath, and took it to the river, where we used it as a boat, then all of us tried to float on it, all 5 of us!. I was not surprised it sank on its first voyage, and we all got wet. Even so, now already wet we salvaged the bath and then attempted the exercise again. They were such fun times playing in the woods, not a care in the world. You really don't know what you had, when you were just about 12 years old, until you grow up and look back retrospectively.

My childhood was undeniably proper in every meaning of the word, a real proper job, and I loved every moment of it. Furthermore, It was a privilege, to have spent a great deal of my childhood, growing up in that pretty country setting that represented so much to me. Mum and dad worked so hard, and looked after us so well, I am 52 years old now, and as I write this it brings back memories so clear of dad and mum. Furthermore, of all the fun times we use to have while living in the cottage, and I miss mum and dad so much now.

Mum is going to take Christine and me to St Ives today, I have not been there since January, when I went with Joe. Its now mid July and the town would have had its annual influx of holiday makers, so will be very busy. We catch the local bus to Penzance station, and then get the direct bus to St Ives, it takes about 35 to 40 minute depending on traffic of course. The bus takes you through Longrock, and past St Erth railway station, among other places on the way. Then it takes the road through Lelant, and Carbis Bay, finally arriving at The Malakoff bus station in St Ives.

We get off the bus and look for a pasty shop for our dinner, mum buys us a pasty and a coke each. Next, we take our dinner to the Harbour, and sit and eat it while watching people swimming with a seal that came into the Harbour. Seals come into the harbour quite frequently, they follow fishing boats back from a days fishing, in hope of a free feed of fish. If you want to see lots of seals, you can take a trip out to sea, where many seals are found on an island, seal island. Seagulls are every where, and are also hoping for a free meal like the seals. Around the Harbour can be seen many artists, with their easels, painting the beautiful views, it's such a wonderful place to come to paint.

After our meal we walk along to the amusement arcade, Christine right away is placed aboard the wooden horse ride, she loves it. We must have played on everything, and then we finish off by playing on the shove a penny machine. Next, mum takes us to Porthminster Beach, a lovely sandy beach, and quite a big one. I love this beach, and little do I know that in around 9 years from now, I will meet my future wife Kim here. Because in the future I will be sunbathing, and my wife Kim actually trips over my legs, and now 32 years later were even more in love. We stay on the beach for a few hours, and then go to get Fish and chips for tea.

After we had our chips, we go for a tour of all the shops in the town, take a walk around the Harbour. Next, its back we go to the Malakoff bus station to catch the bus back home. That was a great day out, and I can't wait for the next time, St Ives always delivers so much, and no wonder so many go there each year, for a holiday. We arrive back at home and tell dad all about our great day out, I play with Christine for a while, and then its time for bed.

The next morning I helped dad in the garden, pushing the wheel burrow around and raking up the weeds he had cut down. I piled them up ready for burning at the back of the cottage, and then Christine and me played for a few hours. Later in the afternoon, we went to Newlyn with mum for a walk. On the way we went by the pilchard works, here the old Cornish tradition of preserving pilchards in salt in wooden casks is performed.

The tradition of salting pilchards goes back to the 1550s, and one of the buyers is a family in Italy, who are also distributors, the factory in Newlyn started production in 1927. Once pilchards arrive at the works, they are cured in salt for any time between four weeks and three years, next pressed of oil and water, and packed in 25 kilo wooden caskets.

We walk on, and past the fish market, were heading towards Penlee quarry, it's quite a nice walk, heavy truck's carrying stone go by us on the way. We have walked many times to Mousehole, the road gives nice views of Mounts Bay all the way along. I love it when we get to Penlee quarry, you actually walk through part of the works on the way. There are large hoppers, where the stone from the quarry drops into, and then is either taken away by trucks, or the little trains I wrote about earlier. Its very dusty, easy to get some grit into your eyes, so we cover our faces with a hanky.

The big trucks with their yellow cabs, thunder by us and turn right into the quarry itself. The best bit for me, is that around midday every day, they blast rock, and it's almost that time now, so we move away. We position our selves further along the Road, and then hear the familiar siren, warning of the blasting. Next, the ground beneath us trembles as a loud explosion rings out around us, and in the distance you can just hear falling rock. All manners of birds are flying by us now, scared by the blast, you would think the birds would have gotten use to it by now.

We continue our walk, and the next place that we come across is Penlee point, and the lifeboat station, which was opened, I believe in 1913, the boat is launched off a ramp and straight into the sea in Mounts bay. Almost in Mousehole now, the home of the Christmas lights that Christine and me love so much. When we arrive, we walk around the Harbour, and mum buys us some sweets. We sit on the beach and with it being summer, there is quite a few people already here. There is a small beach in the harbour when the tides out, and people sit on it, among boats now left high and dry between tides.

Its fun sitting here on the Harbour beach, Christine and myself play, hide and seek behind the boats, being careful not to slip over the ropes attached to them. Many holiday makers come to Mousehole each year, it's such a beautiful place, and many interesting things to offer. Before we head back for home, mum takes us to the bird sanctuary, we walk up the hill to the sanctuary then start looking inside the large cages.

Many birds have had sanctuary here over the years, and the biggest amount of birds in one time was of course due to the oil tanker incident. I look in the cages with Christine, I can see seagulls, black birds, and many other types, they make quite a noise all of them together. Its so funny to see the fit birds looking from outside, into the cages. They, look down at the ill ones, I guess they would like to get some of the food they can see. I spoke to a lady about the birds, and she asks me to come into the food preparation area. It was so very interesting, she had lots of fish in there for the birds, and medicine, and some little chicks. I thanked her, and then mum said it was time to go home, and we walked to the bus stop.

We caught the bus back to Newlyn, and then walked up the Coombe, dad was just finishing the gardening when we arrived at the front gate. Tibby, also greeted me, and I went and got him a bowl of milk. Later me and Christine took him outside to play with us, and he got himself tangled up in a ball of wool. I had to cut Tibby out of the mess he'd gotten himself into, using mums scissors, what a picture he would have made.

I hear the loud sound of motor bikes going by our gate, and see at least 30 bikes go by, on route to Lands End. This was a regular occurrence, many Rockers would make trips to lands End back in the 60s. We had the Mods and Rockers, with Mods riding around on Motor scooters and Rockers riding around on motor bikes in the late 60s. I heard on the news that these two groups would clash from time to time, in particularly in Brighton. I saw lots of bikes and scooters being ridden around back then, with the Motor bike boys all dressed up in leather clothing, and the Mods with their Scooters covered in mirrors, and wearing parker coats. I hope that when I grow up that I will be able to buy a motor bike, they look so cool.

Well, another day closed, and the next day I went out with my friends, we all went to Longrock beach. Longrock is just outside of Penzance and near to Marazion, it gives wonderful views of St Michaels Mount, and Mounts Bay. It's also the base of the world's longest running scheduled helicopter service, and the helicopter fly's its passengers from here to the Isles of Scilly, and has done since 1964. While sitting on the beach, you hear the helicopter preparing to take off, and once airborne it passes's above you, heading out to sea. It makes quite a lot of noise when taking off, and very exciting to watch, its so low I can see the passengers looking out of the windows.

After playing on the beach with my friends we all head off for Penzance, and along to the Ross bridge, we stop there and watch boats landing sharks on the slipway. We take a closer look and one of my mates nearly gets his hand bitten off. The sharks are still quite alive, but don't look like it, it frightens the life out of him, we all laugh. We then play tag along Penzance docks, and get told off by the Harbour master. Next we move to Battery rocks, and sit on the wall watching people in the bathing pool, and wave to some of our friends in there.

Then we head for the Prom, and we put our wet swimsuits back on, the tide is in so we can now do dives from off the railings. We, of course were showing off to the holiday makers, many stopped and watched us. Next, we took it in turn to balance on the railings and dive into the sea. Its quite rough today so we really have to be careful that were not smashed into the wall. A favourite game of ours, was to throw a single large silver coin into the sea, and then, spend many dives seeing who could find it, and bring it back up from the seabed.

We did this quite a lot in summer, some times holiday makers threw coins in the sea for us to get, and we made quite a bit of money for sweets. We would share the money we managed to get, and brought some sweets with it. Finally, we would walk up Love lane, back to Alverton, where I then walked up the hill, and then down to Trereife Lodge.

That night I lay in bed, thinking that soon the summer would be over, and I would be starting in my new school. During the day with my friends, we had once again shared some of our fears regarding our new school. I, of course only had information from my friends older brothers and sisters, that had been passed on to them. The info thus far, is nothing but bad news, it sounds like were in for a hard time soon. I hope it's all hype, but somewhere deep within I know that's not going to be the case.

The next day, mum takes me and Christine to Penlee park, to play on the swings and slides, I take my football along. This park will be found at the top of Morrob Road, and is just behind the library. It's the home of the Open Air Theatre, that seats around 200 people, which had its first season in the early 50s. A very large park, with a large pond just behind the playground section. When we arrive, I push Christine up and down on the swings, play seesaw with her, and play football. The park is full of conker trees, but it's a little to early in the year yet for those. Next, off to the town centre, where mum buys us fish and chips for dinner.

After we ate our fish and chips, we went to Penzance bus station, and caught a bus back home. I went up to my bedroom, and built a puppet theatre out of a cardboard box, and recorded some funny noises, on my reel to reel tape recorder. I then gathered up all my toy puppets, and my special torch that had three coloured lights. Next I made a curtain from two old pillow cases, and finally went down stairs to the front room.

I set my theatre up, and then wrote out a pretend ticket, I gave Christine a call, and when she came into the front room, I gave her a free ticket to my show. She of course was the only member of the audience, but a very willing one. I hid behind the large box, and Donald duck was first to star, and Christine laughed when he appeared. Donald, then waved to her, and said "what's your name?", and Christine replied "Christine", and with that, the show began.

Throughout the show Christine sat mesmerised at the puppets, I had also included her favourite teddy bear, in the cast along with Bongo her big toy dog. I shone my torch on the puppets, and lit their faces up, and for effect, I played funny sounds from my tape recorder that I recorded earlier. The best bit was when I called Christine over to take a surprise gift out of Donald ducks hand, because he handed her a sweet I had saved for her, and it made her so excited. For many days after this, Christine would ask me to have another show, and we had many more.

The next day I went with my friends to Buryas Bridge, there was woods near there, and if you followed the river it would lead you right up to Drift Dam. We use to climb trees while playing tag, and ran around like headless chickens like you did at that age. We walked along the river bank to the dam, and it was impressive to see the power of the water crashing down into the river below. I can recall there's a very long deep stretch of water right below the dam, and that it leads to a deep pool. I saw very large trout swimming in this piece of river, but have never fished this river with Pete. Drift Dam is just a short distance from the little village of Sancreed, and St Buryan is not far away from there either.

Another favourite local myth and legend, that's close to St Buryan, is about The Merry Maidens, dad told me the following about them. Dad told me that the nineteen stones in the field were said to be nineteen maidens. They, had been dancing in a circle, but they were punished for dancing on a Sunday. The punishment had been the maidens were turned to stone where they stood. Near to the maidens are two megaliths, thought to be the two musicians also turned to stone for playing on a Sunday.

Anyway, by the end of our day in the woods I was well tired, and when I got back, I had a quick clean up, watched television for a short time, and then went to bed early. The next day Joe and myself went to Sennen, Joes dad drove us there and said he would pick us up around tea time. This beach is awesome, and is renowned for surfing, and as such has a huge amount of surfers each year.

I go to Sennen a lot, mostly these days with my friends, we mainly use just belly boards, I like riding in the waves just on my belly sometimes. I can remember seeing lots of tents hidden in long grass along the headland around Sennen back then. It was a remarkable time, and the surf scene was well and truly happening in many places in Cornwall. Joe and I, watched guys on huge long boards surfing even bigger waves, Sennen was and still is one of the places to surf.

The beach is packed out today, it now being around mid August, we move our towels and belongings closer to the sea, and put on our masks and snorkels. Entering the surf the waves are quite big, so we stay close to the shore. We manage to see quite a few fish, swimming around the rocks, and sand eels flash as the sun hits their reflective skins. Next we take our masks off and get our belly boards, and ride the waves for at least an hour more. Then we dry our selves, and eat the pack lunches we had brought, the wind is really whipping up the sand, so we put our towels over our heads. The gusts are getting stronger, so Joe and me move further back up the beach, to get out of the wind and find a spot just besides the beach shop.

Joes dad arrives, and takes us back home, being such a beautiful sunny day, I spend the rest of it in our back garden. I love this cottage, and the waterfall besides it, living in the country is everything to me, its peaceful and relaxed. I like to sit, and just watch my dad working in the garden, admiring his strength, and hope I may be strong like that one day. Life was so different when at home, away from the hustle and bustle of Town life, apart from birds or the odd car going by. The best thing about living in the country was, if you sat and listened you would hear nothing just the trickle of the water fall.

The remainder of my summer holiday soon came to an end, and I have made arrangements to meet my friends by the ropewalk in Alverton tomorrow. Next We will carry on to the bus stop, which is just across the road from Alverton shops. When I got home later on, from playing with my friends, mum gave me my dinner, and I had a bath, and then it was an early night to bed. Just before I got into bed, mum came in gave me a kiss, and said, don't worry about the new school, you're my little big man, and every thing will be fine.

I did not sleep that night, tossing and turning, worrying about the new school, and when I got up for breakfast the next day, I felt terrible, I was tired, and of course scared. I had my breakfast mum gave me a big kiss at the gate, and then I walked up my Go - Cart hill, my faithful old test site, for my cart. I had with me, my new big brown satchel, that was strapped on my shoulder. I looked back at mum, and wished so much, that she could have gone in with me on my first day. This was it, the day had come, I am now a little big man in mums eyes at least. I will endeavour to live up to what my mum called me that day, I will work hard to truly be her Little big man.

I met David at the top of the ropewalk, and we walked down to the bus stop, we could see quite a large group of people there. When we finally got to the bus stop, there was a lot of pushing and shoving going on, so we tried to keep out of the way. Some of the older boys were swearing, and an elderly lady and a man going by, told them to stop, but only got an abusive reply back. I must admit I was scared at this point, so was David, although we did not tell each other so. When the bus pulled up, the driver warned some of the boys not to muck about. We decided to go up stairs to sit, and when the bus drove off, some boys stood up, and threw blotting paper laced with ink at pedestrians below. Some of the older girls screamed most of the time through the window at passers by.

Then in no time at all we arrived in Penzance, we got off the bus and headed to the town centre to get some sweets. Next we walked up Causeway Head, crossed the road at the top, and then continued on to school. On arriving at school, we just hung around in the playground, and played in our own little group. Nevertheless, being only year one boys we were considered soft targets for the older boys. Furthermore, before long my group of friends were getting a little attention, but we pretended not to notice. I then needed to go to the toilet, so we all set off to the toilets.

When we got to the outside loo's, to our horror, we had walked in on some poor lad being stretched over a wooden support that held up the roof. He was screaming in pain, four big boys had one limb each, and had suspended him in the air against the wooden post. They ceased doing this to the boy when they noticed we had walked in, the young boy was glad to see us of course. We needless to say had the quickest pee ever, and were out of there in no time.

Well, before long a bell was rung, which meant we had to go to an assembly, and the whole playground made a mad rush for the door. Once inside we mustered in the school hall, and the headmaster addressed us all, we then had to sing a hymn and say the lords prayer. This was not an easy feat, when people were being thumped and pushed behind, and in front of you. After the assembly, everyone moved to their first lesson, and roll call would be carried out first. With us being all new, we were given a guided tour of the school, and given various bits of documentation. half way through the morning, we went out to the playground, and lined up in front of a lady, who gave us a third of a pint of milk each. Then back to our lessons, after about a fifteen minute break.

Dinner time came around very quick, and in the dining area each table had around 8 boys and girls mixed, with a teacher at the end of it. The teacher would let us know when it was our turn to go up. We would then go up and be served by the dinner ladies, go back to our seat, and have to wait for all to return. Then the teacher would ask us to say grace, and choose one of us to speak it, and when Dinner was over, we were then allowed to go and play in the playground.

I saw a lot of bullying in my days at school, and it was hard work to say the least to stay out of bother. We hung around in our own group, but many times my friends were picked on and beat up. I was lucky enough to stay out of the way, but on three occasions was forced to fight or fall, I chose to stay on my feet, I am glad to say. I tried very hard to study in my lessons, but our classes were disrupted all the time by a lot of the class. Our lessons always had around 42 pupils in it, and many children very totally disruptive.

During lessons it was normal to see paper planes flying around the classroom, pea shooters being used, certain children swearing and being abusive at the teacher. In addition, even threatening to arm the teacher, I found it a scary place to be most of the time, and longed for the 5 years to rapidly pass. It was nothing more than a sentence, not schooling, it was a place I feared, and I am angry that my education was rubbish on account of it. I wanted to learn, I wanted to learn so bad, but it was near on impossible to achieve in that environment.

Every night on leaving school, there was always some poor lad being surrounded by a ring of boys, while another was beating him up. Furthermore, the bus home was a repeat performance of the pandemonium of the early morning. I was so glad to get back home to normality, mum asked if I had a nice day, and I said it was great. However, the reality was that all my friends and myself fears, during summer holidays turned out to be correct.

The nights had grown darker by now, so I was not allowed out to play after around Seven o'clock. So, it was a bit of Television and then a bath and off to bed on weekdays, would have rather stayed up of course. On one occasion when going to school, my friends, and I were chased down to the bus stop by a group of older boys. Who, just laughed at us when we got to the bus stop, we were really spooked that day. Despite all this, I really enjoyed metal work at school, and geography, history, and my favourite lesson was science. It was just hard to concentrate with the disruptions.

My second day at school was tougher, when in the assembly a bigger boy than me stood on my toe by mistake, but suddenly found it funny. Next, he followed me outside, and pushed me from behind, and said he was going to rough me up, I asked why, and he said because he could. Then, lucky for me a mate of his said leave the lad go, and that I was only a first year, and he did. Life at school was full of little disruptions, every single day, and you had to learn to live with them, and I soon found that being diplomatic helped a lot.

In the playground we played British Bulldog a lot of the time, and tag, we were always told off repeatedly for running by the teachers. If you were told more than once you would be kept back after school, and made to write out, I must Not run in school 500 times. I got the cane in my first year, and it was very painful, and I did not do any thing wrong. I had been talking in class to my friend, and the teacher told me to stop, someone behind me laughed and the teacher thought it had been me. So, I was marched off to the headmasters study, and waited for what seemed an age, then the headmaster told me to come in.

He told me I was about to learn a lesson today regard-ing manners, I was scared and wished I could just dis-appear. Next, he shouted "Hold out your hand ", I did, and then he brought the cane down hard across the palm of my hand, and two more followed. It was so un-fair, protesting your innocence would have been a com-plete waste of time, and if you got your dad to come to school to speak to the headmaster, you would have been beaten up for grassing.

My big school fears had been correct, the stories I had heard, in know ways prepared me for this place. I could not feel relaxed enough to absorb any lessons, in the early days of my new school. My friends were of course in the same predicament to, and we talked in the playground about how rubbish it was. Looking back on it, I feel in my opinion that the teachers let me and my friends down, and that my education suffered due to it.

You should be able to go to school, and work in an environment that complements your efforts, not in a hostile one like the one my friends, and I had to bear. There was also a culture, of everyone was to blame for one persons misgivings, totally unfair. If someone did not own up for some act carried out behind the teachers back, he would keep the whole class back after school ends. This happened over and over again, and of course we always knew who it had been, but to say it would have meant a certain beating. If you protested that it was not you, and that it was not fair, the teacher would keep you in the next day, and the rest of the class. Which you can imagine, would have made you very popular, especially with the bad guys.

Instead of me wishing to achieve at school, I ended up wishing for every year to end soon so I could escape. All my ambitions that I had thought about, evaporated the day I went to this school. I reckon, I did well only because I studied more at home, than I did at school, I owe this to my encyclopaedias I had and homework. I did try of course, I tried hard in all my lessons, but it was just impossible to concentrate, you had to put up with paper planes, other things being thrown around, chairs being kicked, abuse being directed at the teacher. Don't get me wrong, I know this happens in schools, but this was nearly every day in every class. Furthermore, all the teachers did, most of the time, was to punish the whole class on account of one half of the class being bad.

The fun happy days of primary school melt away like they never existed, and my heart feels empty, this new school for the next 5 years of my life, will mould me ready for adult life!. I was stunned at the stark difference between this school and my last, and begin to wonder what in the long run will become of me, I am only 11 years old. It's such a big change, and nothing prepares you for it, one minute you're a happy go lucky child and then in the same year you are in mainstream school. This new school was huge in comparison to my last, the amount of pupils to a class were double at around 42 to a classroom. Furthermore, a large amount of the children here, were from huge housing estates and I up until then, had little or no contact with these huge communities, and had lived quite a sheltered life in the country.

With such deep feelings about school life affecting me, I did actually approach mum, one night just before I went to bed, I called mum up to my room. I told her that I was finding it very hard in the new school, and that I was scared most of the time. Mum said it was quite normal to feel this way, and that I was to give it time. I gave her a big kiss, but knew in my heart, that it was not just because it was a new experience. I never approached her again with my feelings, I just knuckled down and got on with it.

The fundamental problem for me was, I was picked on for being a country boy, which hurt a lot, because I loved the country life. Country life, was my whole way of life at this point of time, and I loved it. However, soon a new problem will emerge for me, because my family, one day soon will leave our lovely cottage, and move to a council estate. This move, will make my life a complete hell, because I come from the country I get picked on big time from gangs. This move I write more about in my next book, so, please keep an eye on my website.

I enjoyed my life growing up in our little cottage in Trereife, living by the woods. I loved Fishing for the Big one with my brother Pete, and of having had the Privilege to have been born and bred in Cornwall. Cornwall is a beautiful place, and is full of wonderful people who look forward to giving you a warm welcome some day. Therefore, if you have never been, I would urge you to pay a visit, whether for a day or a week, you won't leave disappointed.

This is where I will leave this part of my childhood, I hope that the book will be read by many people, and that I can write the second part. The next book will cover my childhood from 12 to 18 years old growing up in Cornwall. Our family later moved to Newlyn In the 70s, I really hope you have enjoyed my book, and maybe I have reminded many of you of this same period in your own childhood back in the 1960s.

A Recipe for you to Try

Cornish Pasty

Ingredients to make short crust pastry

Approx 453 Grams of plain flour
Approx 227 Grams of either butter or margarine or a mix of both
Milk or cold water to mix according to your preference
One good pinch of salt

Method

We like to put the flour through a sieve first, then add the salt, cut the fat up into very small pieces. Next rub together well, until the fat is no longer lumps, but try not to make it to fine. Next mix in some water or milk slowly, or a mix of both liquids, and mix it altogether until you can form a ball of dough. Try not to make it to wet or sticky. Then you need to allow this to rest for a while, in a cool area, we tend to leave it in a bowl with a tea towel over the top of the bowl in a cool place in the kitchen.

The ingredients required for the filling.

Approx 340 Grams Good lean beef
1 large Potato.

1 small Swede/or could be called turnip.
1 small onion, we prefer a red one.
Salt and Pepper to personal tastes.
Approx 28 Grams of butter.

Preparation

Wash and clean all the vegetables, make sure the fat is left out the fridge for some time, to make it easy to rub into the flour.

Beat 1 egg in to a small dish, in preparation for an egg washing the pastry, this helps the pasties to be brown when baking.

Get a baking tray, rub some fat on to it until the tray is covered, then sprinkle some flour on to the tray. Then shake the flour around so it sticks to the fat, finally shake of all the excess flour. This will now stop your pasty from sticking to the tray after its been baked.

Place about half an egg cup of water to one side.

Some flour to dust the dough rolling out area.

Next the meat, cut this into small bits, say about a sugar cube size.

A rolling pin.

A pastry brush.

A knife to cut up the cleaned vegetables.

Salt and pepper

A small amount of milk in an eggcup.

Method

First cut all your vegetables into small pieces, I like mine to be quite thin, and not to long, it cooks quicker, so about 2.5 cm long, and 1.5 cm thick, it's up to you on the size.

Now sprinkle some flour on to the table, ready for you to roll out the dough.

Next roll your dough out into a circle shape, about dinner plate size, and make the thickness be a little bigger than $^3/_4$ of a cm.

Dampen the sides of this dough shape, with some milk, this will help seal it when crimping the sides later. Now put half of the dough over the rolling pin, so that you have the other half on the table ready to fill.

Now fill that half with the vegetables, and then place the cuts of meat across the vegetables, next, sprinkle the salt and pepper to your own tastes over the vegetables and meat.

Then using a little of the water you have put aside, throw a little of that over the mix. Next take the butter, and lay this in bits across the whole mix, finally sprinkle a bit of flour over the mix. This enables the fat and all the juices during baking, to combine to make a rich gravy.

Almost there, now put the other half of the dough that's on the rolling pin, over the mix of ingredients.

Now using your fingers and thumbs, crimp the sides together, you simply work from the right, place your left hands index finger and thumb on the pastry, and your right hands finger and thumb to the right of your left hands finger and thumb. Now, pinch the pastry with your right hand finger and thumb, and bring it up and down onto the pastry, and fold the pastry into a little crimp. Repeat that all the way across, until you reach the end. It's a little hard to describe here, if you can't do it, check it out on the internet, (how to crimp pastry)

Then place the pasty on the prepared baking tray, cut a little hole in the top to let steam escape. Next wash the top with the beaten egg, put some grease proof paper over the top of the pasty, this is to stop it from browning to quickly.

Now place in the cooker in the middle, and bake at 220 centigrade for 20 to 25 minutes, and then, remove grease proof paper and drop temperature to around 160 centigrade, and leave to bake for another 40 minutes. Use a meat skewer to check the inside of the pasty to see if its nearly cooked.

Now relax and enjoy your Cornish pasty.

Please watch out for more books I will be writing in the future, these will be found on my website below.

www.Mikedarracott.com